Greece

a handbook for Christian visitors

By
John Hayden

Honey Hill Publishing

Honey Hill Publishing
St Mary's Church, Honey Hill, Bury St Edmunds, Suffolk IP33 1RT, UK

Quotations from the Bible are taken from the New International Version (USA edition) and are used by permission of the copyright holders, the International Bible Society, Colorado Springs, USA.
ISBN 978–0–9554504–3–3

Honey Hill Publishing is an enterprise of St Mary's Church, Bury St Edmunds, Suffolk, UK.

Contents

Introduction

The aim of this book is to give a handy guide to those visiting Greece on a pilgrimage. No attempt is made to replace the excellent guidebooks like the *Footprints* series or, for that matter, the commentary of the local guides.

A vast amount of information is now available on the World Wide Web and anyone visiting these venues would profit from reading the entries in Wikipedia and other sites. In this short handbook I am not attempting to compete with such a mass of information.

However, I am trying, almost in note form, to bring together key facts that enable any pilgrim to get a real feel for the sites that are visited.

There are many very good commentaries covering the Acts of the Apostles and the letters to the various churches. I am not attempting to provide such a commentary but to highlight key passages in these New Testament books which refer to the Graeco-Roman culture of the day. The aim is to help pilgrims feel they are in the shoes, or more likely sandals, of those in the days of Paul.

So it is important to read a good commentary in order to understand the biblical teaching of these passages. Probably the best small commentaries are the *Crossway Bible Guides*. They not only give an easy-to-read commentary on the text but also have many short articles covering matters like, Who were the Judaizers? It is also worth searching for commentaries online or in electronic format.

Finally my very grateful thanks to Lance Bidewell for his meticulous editing and proof reading which as usual became a massive task.

Bishop John Hayden 2010

Background

A brief history of Greece

In the first century AD, Greece was administered by the Romans as the provinces of Achaea in the south and Macedonia in the north.

Achaea By the third millennium BC the Aegean area was under the influence of Minoan (Cretan) culture and was the most developed area of Europe. As the second millennium approached, the area was under increasing pressure from invasion by the Achaeans invading from the north. Other invaders included the Ionians and Aeolians, as well as Dorians who moved down from Epirus. The Dorians with their iron weapons conquered large areas and put the area culturally back into a dark age.

Individual city states began to emerge, with the population able to flee into the acropolis (fortified high area) of the city in times of invasion. Argos and Mycenae tended to dominate and the Mycenaean culture began to bring Greece back into civilization. Although these city states normally acted independently, by 800 BC they were collectively known as the Hellenes. Most cities developed through a political pattern between 800 and 600 BC, with kings first of all replaced by aristocratic ruling families (oligarchs) and then through various unlawful means by tyrants drawn from the dissatisfied wealthy classes. During this time Sparta began to rival Athens and built up its own league of cities.

By 500 BC Athens was under democratic rule and used its power to assist local states in their revolt against Persian rule. In 492 Darius tried to exact tribute but Athens and Sparta refused to pay. In 490 Miltiades of Athens repulsed a much larger Persian army. In 480 the Persians' massive army marched through Greece and, in spite of valiant resistance by the Spartans, reached Athens and destroyed the city. However, at sea the much smaller Greek fleet was victorious and within a year the Persians were forced to leave Greece. Culturally the centre for ancient art and learning moved from Asia Minor (under Persian rule) to Athens.

The removal of the Persians just led to increased warfare between Athens (with its dominant fleet) and Sparta with its superior army. Eventually Sparta gained the upper hand and for many years there were constant wars between the various city states. By 370 a new power, Thebes, had taken over from Sparta but their rule only lasted eight years. Constant infighting in the south allowed the Kingdom of Macedonia to advance. Alexander died in 323 BC and rivalries between the states began yet again. Rome took this opportunity to increase its influence and won an important battle in 196 BC. The Greeks tried to revolt, but in 146 BC Roman legions under Lucius Mummius took Corinth and abolished the city states. The Greeks revolted again and in 86 BC the Romans sacked Athens. Led by Sulla, they left most of Greece in ruins. Athens remained a centre for philosophy but it had no political power.

In the second century AD Athens revived under the Emperor Hadrian and the Greek Herodes Atticus and much rebuilding took place in Athens and other cities. In spite of its political instability the Achaean area remained an important centre for trade in agriculture and minerals. In Roman times many professionals like doctors and teachers came from Greece and its works of art were in popular demand.

Macedonia Macedonia basically was a buffer state between the Greeks in the south and the many European tribes in the north. Macedonians were looked upon by the Greeks as barbarians because they did not adopt the city-state concept and much of the culture of the south. There were groups of Greek-speaking peoples in Macedonia: the Ionians in Thessaly, and Aeolians in eastern Macedonia, and the Macedones in the west from which the region takes its name.

The kingdom of Macedonia was firmly established in the seventh century BC but it did not exert much influence on the region until the reign of Philip II, who came to power in 359 BC. By the year of his assassination in 336 BC most of Greece was under his control.

His young son Alexander the Great took up his father's plans to defeat the Persians, which he did in 333 and 331 BC, bringing the whole of the Persian Empire under Macedonian control. His empire stretched as far as Egypt and the borders of India but he died in 323 BC and his conquests were divided among his generals. In less than forty years the Macedonian Empire rose and fell, yet its influence lasted many centuries. This is because Alexander's generals had much more influence in the lands to the east of Greece, while the power of Macedonia rapidly collapsed. Rome, by 146 BC, had taken over complete control and Macedonian independence was lost. It remained part of the Roman and Byzantine Empires until the eleventh century AD and the fall of Constantinople.

In the first century AD the prosperity of Macedonia depended on the major trade route – the Via Egnatia and the founding of Roman colonies like Philippi. There were vast arable and livestock farms run by very wealthy ruling families making use of slave labour. There was a large export surplus through its thriving ports as well as along the Via Egnatia. Such trade attracted a considerable Jewish population and traders like Lydia from Thyatira, who would have had a major market for her luxury cloth.

Architecture

Greek 700 — 146 BC

Greek architecture of the Hellenic Period has long been recognized as the most beautiful building form yet devised by man. The essentially simple column and beam method of construction formed the basis of this style of architecture, which was used for all temples and important public buildings. This style is thought to have been derived from timber construction methods. The columns, beams and other components were stylized and refined by succeeding generations of artists and craftsmen to a degree which has rarely been equalled and never surpassed in the building forms of subsequent ages.

Marble was readily available for constructing the most important buildings, and the natural beauty of this material, carved with great skill into the structurally pure and well proportioned forms of Greek temples glistening white under cloudless Mediterranean skies, must have afforded a sight of awesome beauty, making it easy to believe that the gods had made their homes on earth.

Greek temples, although basically similar in general shape and construction, nevertheless differed in detail and ornament. Three main types are evident: namely the Doric, Ionic and Corinthian Orders. These are chiefly distinguished from each other by the proportions of the columns and the shapes of the column tops or capitals.

The earliest, simplest and most robust style is the Doric, with examples dating from 640 BC. The most famous temple built in this style is the Parthenon at Athens, constructed in the period from 447 to 432 BC.

The Ionic Order, with examples dating from 560 BC, has columns of a more slender proportion than the Doric and can easily be identified by the remarkable volute, or scroll, design of the capitals.

The Corinthian dates from 420 BC. The slender columns are topped by an inverted bell shape surrounded by acanthus leaves.

Roman 146 BC — AD 365

Remains of buildings dating from the Roman period are to be found at many of the ancient city sites of Asia Minor and Greece. Roman architecture owes much to the Greeks and also the Etruscans who were the original inhabitants of Central Italy. Their architecture, dating from about 750 BC, is specially notable for the use of the radiating arch, and the Romans continued to use this form, combined with the column and beam favoured by the Greeks. This combination of columns and beams with arches and vaults gives Roman architecture its own distinctive character.

The Doric, Ionic and Corinthian Orders continued to be used by the Romans, who also added two other types, namely the Tuscan and the Composite. The Tuscan is a simplified version of the Doric with an unfluted shaft, simple moulded capital and plain entablature. The Composite has a capital which is a combination of the Corinthian and Ionic types and was often used in triumphal arches to give an ornate character.

Temples were the predominant buildings of the Greeks and were of one storey, but the complex civilization and varied needs of the Romans demanded other buildings, often of several storeys. Thermae (baths), temples, amphitheatres, aqueducts, bridges, tombs and basilicas all testify to the great constructive ability of the Romans, whose majestic buildings were in accord with the grandeur of Roman Imperial power.

The Romans invented a form of concrete which they used to great effect and economy in the construction of walls, vaults and domes. Brick, stone, marble and mosaic were still used, but only as facing materials.

Mosaics were used not only on walls but on floors and are of great variety. Statues housed in niches in walls were much in use as decoration.

Temples were similar in general form to Greek temples, although half columns attached to the side walls often took the place of the surrounding colonnade of the Greeks. Roofs were often vaulted. They were generally sited to face onto the public open space or forum. A few temples, such as the famous pantheon in Rome, were built in circular form.

Basilicas were halls of justice and commercial exchange. The usual plan of a basilica was a rectangle twice as long as its width. Two or four rows of columns divided the interior into three or five aisles. The tribunal was at the far end on a raised dais, set in a semicircular apse around which were ranged seats for the assessors. The basilica form is interesting, in that it was adopted by the early Christians as a pattern for church buildings, after Christianity was permitted as a public religion in the fourth century AD.

Greek Capitals

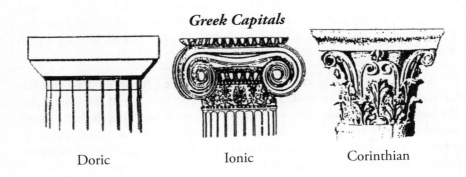

Doric   Ionic   Corinthian

Roman Capitals

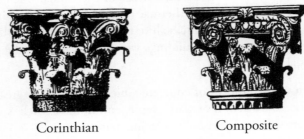

Corinthian   Composite

Three examples of Byzantine capitals

Greek Philosophy

It is interesting that Greek philosophy began in the eastern cities of Ionia, Asia Minor, and then spread into Greece. These early philosophers were influenced by thinking from China, India, Persia and Egypt.

Thales (640-550 BC) and the early philosophers focused on the substance of which all things are composed. For Thales it was water in all its forms.

Anaximander (611-547) taught that the primary elements of earth, water, air and fire came from the 'unlimited' or 'indeterminate'.

Pythagoras

Pythagoras (570-500) brought together religion and philosophy. He stressed the importance of form and proportion. His view is expressed in the phrase 'all things are numbers', meaning geometrical figures. (*illus.*)

Xenophanes (570-480) founded the Eleatic School which attacked those like Homer who gave an anthropomorphic concept of the gods. He believed in one supreme god who was not like man in body or thought.

Parmenides (540-480) claimed nothing could come into being out of nothing, so reality is eternal.

Zeno (490-420) showed the absurdity in pluralism that reality is a multiplicity.

Heraclitus (540-475) focused on fire as the key matter. Matter is always changing but its source is fire. He also taught the reality of universal reason and law. (*illus.*)

Heraclitus

Anaxagoras (500-428) taught that 'intelligence' had sorted out the matter of the universe from a multiplicity of seeds. He brought Ionian philosophy to Athens.

Democritus (460-370) taught that atoms and space are the only ultimate realities. Objects differ because of size, shape and position but are all made up of atoms. All worlds come about by the joining of atoms. Beside atoms there is no other reality.

Socrates (469-399) was more interested in the problems of human behaviour than in ultimate realities. He believed in the possibility of knowledge which when checked by observable facts could form valid concepts. He died as the first philosophy martyr. As he left nothing in writing his ideas were interpreted in a variety of ways. Some taught that pleasure was the highest good. Others, impressed by his hardships, preached the simple life. Euclid was sceptical about the validity of the senses.

Plato

Plato (427-347) opened a school in Athens in 387. He agreed with Heraclitus that objects on earth are in constant change, so no truth can be without the possibility of change. However, there were eternal forms. What we observe on earth is a poor imitation of these ultimate forms. The essence of the universe is 'the good'. In his *Republic* he sought to eliminate anything that was substandard and laid the roots for the Nazi attitude towards those mentally or physically ill. (*Illus.*)

Aristotle (384-322) was probably the most important Greek philosopher and his writings still form the basis of most aspects of the subject. The base of his philosophy rests on the concepts of matter and form. He accepted Plato's concept of other-world forms but felt that the idea of these being 'copied' on earth was just a metaphor. His frustration is easy to understand if we think of Plato as a mathematician dealing in concepts, whereas Aristotle was a biologist in a world that can be observed. So Aristotle saw no problem in change and adaptation but the basic essence must remain: for instance, a marble statue cannot change into a man. He did accept 'god' (Plato's 'good') as the final cause of the universe. God is not the creator, as matter is eternal, but he is behind the change and movement, inducing all matter to seek a higher form. (*Illus.*)

Aristotle

Epicurus (341-271) devalued the concept of knowledge to its usefulness in practical situations. A study of human nature can help self-control and a study of the world around can help remove groundless fear and superstition, but theoretical knowledge is of no real use. Pleasure, especially mental pleasure, was supreme as there was no such thing as an eternal soul.

Zeno (336-264) and the Stoics also saw knowledge as an aid to virtue. Their world view was pantheistic and their aim was to live in harmony with all of nature. Rational self-control enabled one to be free and contented.

Pyrrho (360-270) and the sceptics took the line that the human mind was incapable of true knowledge, so it was best to adopt a sceptical neutrality to avoid any tension.

These last three philosophies were similar in their application for day-to-day life. They regarded peace of mind as the highest good we could attain and urged freedom from the circumstances in which we live.

Philo (25 BC – AD 50) and the Neoplatonists were the fruit of the break-down of nationalism throughout the Roman Empire. In Alexandria, the philosophy of the west met with the religion of the east. So Philo of Alexandria tried to harmonize Hebrew religion with Greek philosophy. The ultimate source of all things is god who has endowed into all things a world-soul. This polytheism was readily accepted by the world of his day. Neoplatonists taught that the human soul has fallen and needed a succession of rebirths through training in mysticism and asceticism.

Greek Mythology

Homer is regarded as the key source of information about the Greek gods. The *Iliad* and *Odyssey* were written to be used as entertainment.

The Greek gods were closer to humans in their behaviour than those of other religions. There were differences: for instance, they were ageless and not limited to normal physical body restrictions, so they could go anywhere invisibly. Each deity had his specific functions, and together they lived around Zeus on Mount Olympus. Olympus could be any high mountain but it especially referred to a range between Thessalonica and Larissa.

The key gods are listed below with the Roman names, where appropriate, in brackets.

Zeus

Zeus (Jupiter) was the father of gods, the protector of law and morals and the centre of family life and discipline. However, Zeus had various wives. He was also the sky god and so was seen in lightning and thunder. He was attended by Themis and Nemesis. (*Illus.*)

Hera (Juno), the wife and sister of Zeus and the daughter of Kronos and Rhea, was the patroness of marriage. She had a fierce tongue which even Zeus feared. Her children included Ares, Hebe, and Hephaestus.

Poseidon (Neptune) was the god of earthquakes and the sea. He was the brother of Zeus and unlike the other gods he lived in the ocean depths. He was also the god of dolphins and horses. The Isthmian games were held in his honour.

Apollo was the son of Zeus and Leto and brother of Artemis. For the Greeks he represented the height of manly beauty. His special role was the care of herds and flocks and he was also linked to archery, music and medicine. So he is often pictured with a lyre and a bow.

Artemis (Diana), the twin sister of Apollo, was the goddess of the countryside and wild animals. She was pictured as a virgin huntress and the patron of chastity.

Athena (Minerva) sprang fully grown from the head of Zeus after he had swallowed her mother Metis. She was regarded as the patron goddess of Athens, wisdom and the fine arts.

Hermes (Mercury) was the son of Zeus and Maia. He was portrayed as the messenger of the gods who accompanied the dead to Hades. He was the patron of all who use the roads and was honoured at the roadsides with stone piles (herms). He was a witty person, always up to tricks.

Ares (Mars) was the god of war.

Aphrodite

Aphrodite (Venus) was the goddess of beauty, love and fertility. Born from the sea off Cyprus, she was sex personified and the mother of Eros.

Eros, the god of love, was portrayed as Cupid, a child with a bow and arrow. (*Illus.*)

Hephaestus (Vulcan), the son of Zeus and Hera, was the god of fire and so of craftsmen.

Demeter (Ceres) was the sister of Zeus and the goddess of grain. She was the mother of Persephone.

Dionysus (Bacchus), primarily the god of wine, was also the god of inspiration and all irrational impulses.

Greece in the Bible

Neapolis Acts 16: 6-11

By Paul's day Greece was an area very much in decline. Modern-day Greece was in the Roman Provinces of Achaea and Macedonia in the north. It is not a surprise that Paul in Acts 16 wanted to visit a key centre like Ephesus or go north towards the Black Sea, rather than cross over into the spent force of Greece.

They reached Troas, which was a port about 10 miles south of the ancient city of Troy, and it was in Troas that Paul had the vision of the man from Macedonia urging him to come over to help them. Such visions were common in Paul's day but it is interesting how Luke describes Paul being directed by the Holy Spirit on his journey to Troas and then receiving this vision. Here Luke seems to have joined them We do not know where Luke came from, and some think he was the man of Macedonia.

A T Pierson, in *The Acts of the Holy Spirit,* (MM&S 1895) drew attention to the double guidance of Paul and his fellow travellers. 'on the one hand prohibition and restraint, on the other permission and constraint. They are forbidden in one direction, invited in another; one way the Spirit says "go not"; the other he calls "Come". 'There are many such examples in church history: for instance, Livingstone went to Africa when he had planned to go to China. We could also think of this in terms of negative and positive. If in seeking God's guidance there is a 'no', we should seek for a 'yes'. Here the guidance was such that Paul and his fellow travellers were convinced (v.10) – *symbibazo* means 'put together in one's mind'. Note that God's guidance never bypasses our own mental and spiritual judgment. He urges us to test everything by the principle that nothing the Holy Spirit leads us to do will be contrary to the teaching and character of Jesus.

Neapolis was the port of Philippi, about ten miles to the north-west of Mount Symbolum. It was the eastern end of the Via Egnatia, a key route that ended in Dyrrhachium on the Adriatic. Rome had built this vital west-east route in c.130 BC and made Macedonia a province in 146 BC. By the time of Paul, Macedonia was of vital importance to Rome, and colonies of Roman citizens like Philippi helped protect this key trade route. The journey from Troas to Neapolis only took two days. A later sailing from Neapolis to Troas (Acts 20:6) took five days, which shows how much ancient travel depended on favourable winds.

(See Kavala – page 61)

Philippi Acts 16:12-40

Paul now travels the ten miles along the Via Egnatia to the Roman colony of Philippi.

Philippi had been founded by Philip of Macedon but later became a Roman colony. It had been the scene of the battle in 42 BC between Octavian (later Emperor Augustus) and Mark Antony against Brutus and Cassius, which effectively ended the Roman Republic. A decade later Octavian defeated Antony at the battle of Actium to become the undisputed emperor of the Roman world. Many of Antony's veterans were settled in this new colony that had been given the name Colonia Victrix Philippensium in 42 BC. Roman colonies were strategically sited, and many of its people held Roman citizenship either by birth or granted by a victorious general. In many ways they were garrison towns of reservists, with the Latin language (about 80 per cent of inscriptions there are in Latin, a far higher percentage than elsewhere in the Greek- speaking lands) and way of life set amidst the local Greek architecture and town planning. Other Roman colonies mentioned in the Acts of the Apostles are Corinth, Pisidian Antioch, Iconium, Lystra and Troas. Although Philippi came under Amphipolis, the administrative centre of the district, and Thessalonica the provincial capital of Macedonia, the Roman citizens of Philippi were very proud of their colonial status and Luke emphasizes their claim to being the best city in the area. An attempt to guard their status led to the events of Acts 16:35-40. Some maintain that Luke may have come from Philippi; however, he does not seem to have had either friends with whom to stay or any access to people of influence in the city.

Paul and his companions walked on the Sabbath to the River Gangites, where they had heard that a group was meeting for worship (v.13). The river is about 1.5 miles from the city, which was beyond the Jewish rule for a Sabbath day's journey, so those attending put the importance of worship before the rule-book of their day. Jews and god-fearers often met for worship close to the local river so that it was easy to perform the acts of ritual washing before worship. They found a group of women, so there seem to have been less than ten male Jews to form a synagogue. Paul seems to have engaged them in conversation, as Luke notes that they sat down. Formal teaching was given standing.

Lydia, a dealer in the very expensive purple cloth from Thyratira, was among these worshippers. As Thyratira was a town in the region of Lydia, some have speculated that this was not her real name but one used to help preserve her identity. In the years ahead Lydia and others in Philippi were Paul's main source of income (Philippians 4:15ff). Following her conversion, Lydia was able to provide Paul and his companions with a place to stay in her household. There is no mention of a husband but she could have been married and her husband just kept out of such religious matters. Historians of the time point out that many wealthy women from Asia were followers of religions like Judaism, and Lydia may have come in contact with the fairly large Jewish community in her home town. Being a merchant she most likely had guest accommodation for her suppliers and customers.

The slave girl with a spirit of divination or python (v.16) was not a rare sight in the world of Paul's day. She claimed to be possessed by the god Apollo of Delphi – the snake god. Plutarch tells us that such fortune- telling was often done by the use of ventriloquism, adding even more to the appearance that the god was speaking.

Those who heard her would not be surprised when she talked of the Most High God. They may have associated him with Zeus and possibly even the Jewish God. The concept of the need for salvation was a common theme of the day, especially in the 'mystery' religions which were often adopted by soldiers. Her cries were similar to those which Jesus rebuked in his many encounters with demon-possessed people, e.g. Luke 4:33-34; 8:27-28. Paul had experienced this with Elymas of Cyprus, and followed Jesus' example in commanding the spirit to leave her. Such possession is very rare in the western world but common in other continents. In those places the church still continues a major ministry of exorcism. David Gooding in *True to the Faith* (Hodder 1990) comments: 'spiritism is by definition incompatible with Christianity… for if Paul to have accepted her testimony would have validated her form of spiritism in the eyes of the public. Paul was obliged to demonstrate that the source of the girl's testimony was demonically evil.' For those who heard her, the term 'Most High God' would have meant the local chief deity. The lack of the definite article before 'way of salvation' also compromised Paul's message.

Paul and Silas are dragged before the authorities (*archontes*) in the court area that was situated at one end of the market place or agora. Luke uses the Greek term *strategos* for the Latin praetor or magistrate. Philippi seems to have had two of these men. The charge of proselytizing for foreign gods was a common one and was judged severely. The magistrates saw themselves as defenders of all things Roman but seem to have ignored the fact that the girl had claimed to be possessed by a Greek god. For the Roman citizens of Philippi any attempt to convert their population to Judaism or Christianity would have been interpreted as an attack on emperor-worship and so disloyal to Rome. The accusers built their case on the latent anti-Semitism of the people. Jews usually prospered as merchants and often provoked envious hostility. Recently Claudius had expelled all Jews from Rome. David Gooding comments:

> Callously to exploit the frenzies of a distraught young girl for the sake of making money is unspeakably evil. And to object to her return to sanity because it lost them income, and to raise up public animosity and persecution against the gospel on that ground, is inhumanly wicked…. Shrewdly enough they chose to play on the racial and cultural prejudices of their fellow citizens against the gospel and the evangelists. Now cultural differences and ethnic distinctions are in themselves beautiful things. … But when cultural prejudice blinds people to the gospel it ceases to be the innocent thing it normally is; and when ethnic differences are used to provoke racism and persecution they become self-evidently demonic, as we in this century have cause to know. (*True to the Faith*, Hodder 1990, p.274)

Paul says he was beaten with rods (v.22) three times and we can assume that one of them was at Philippi. The punishment may have been carried out by the lictors (*rhabdouchous*) who carried the ceremonial rods of the praetors. Such beatings were used to obtain evidence, humiliate those concerned, cause injuries that could lead to death, and discourage others from following them. It was against Roman law for such a beating to take place but Paul's and Silas' cry *civis Romanus sum*, affirming their citizenship, may have been either unheard or ignored. Sherwin-White in *Roman Society and Roman Law in the New Testament* (OUP 1963) points out that 'according to the text of the lex Julia…. The Roman citizen might not be beaten or bound by a magistrate *adversus provocationem* or by any other person in any circumstances.' So later the magistrates were forced into a humiliating climbdown, and as they had no power to force

Paul and Silas to leave the city they had to plead with them to move on, probably for their own safety.

The jail may have been in the basement of the jailer's house, as verse 34 mentions that he brought them up into the house, and would be a reason why at the time of the earthquake he was not sleeping by the door of the jail but could reach it soon afterwards.

Earthquakes have always been common in the area. The miracle is that one occurred on that night. As Christians we would claim this was not a coincidence but a God-incidence. Long-term prisoners were a rarity in those days. Prison was a temporary place for those awaiting execution or release after a short while. The jailer thought of committing suicide, knowing that he had under his guard those marked for execution. Paul and Silas, who may not have been among such prisoners, were able to assure him that no one had escaped.

Chrysostom points out 'he washed them and was washed; those he washed from their stripes, himself was washed from his sins.' As the head of the household was responsible for the worship of the gods, the whole household seems to have been baptized into his new faith. Sadly, down the centuries such baptisms have led to nominal Christians. A Roman soldier was not permitted to marry, but the jailer may have been regarded as retired from active service and so able to marry. In that case there may have been young children in the household.

John Stott comments (*Message of Acts,* The Bible Speaks Today, 1990, p.269) that in Philippi we have an account of three people converted from three social backgrounds: the wealthy Lydia, the slave girl and the Roman citizen civil servant. They had their own needs. For Lydia it was intellectual, as she listened she opened her life to Christ. For the girl after the exorcism there was a need for psychological healing from years of abuse as a slave at the whim of her masters. For the jailer it was moral, his conscience had been aroused and he cried out to know how he could be saved. John Stott concludes, 'The wealthy business woman, the exploited slave girl and the rough Roman gaoler had been brought into a brotherly or sisterly relationship with each other and with the rest of the church's members.'

After his first visit in around AD 50, Paul visited Philippi again in AD 56 and 57. His letter to the church was probably written in AD 62.

Letter to the Philippians

Chapter 1 Paul uses the normal wording for opening a letter in the first century. He begins with the name of the writer, the addressee and a greeting. It is one of the few occasions when Paul does not use the title 'apostle'. This is the only church where he does not need to exert his apostolic authority. Indeed he describes himself and Timothy as slaves (*doulos*) of Christ.

The church, whose membership was set apart for God (saints), had developed rapidly and now had bishops, or overseers, and deacons, or helpers. It is probable that the overseers (note they are always referred to in the plural) looked after the spiritual life of the church family, and the deacons, as those appointed in Jerusalem, looked after the practical matters, including the relief of the needy. However, as with Stephen in Acts 7, both roles were seen as having a strong spiritual commitment to Christ.

As part of the formal letter address, Paul substitutes the secular word *chaireis* (greeting) with *charis* (grace) and adds the Hebrew *shalom* (peace).

In his opening remarks Paul uses phrases that would have been very much part of common speech, such as 1:8 calling on a god as a witness. Those who knew the philosophy of the day would likewise relate to teaching about undergoing physical hardship and imprisonment with fortitude. However, he also makes it clear that his teaching, although related to the culture, is transformed in every aspect by the gospel.

We are not sure to whom Paul is referring in 1:13 by the 'whole praetorium'. The NRSV Bible translates this as 'imperial guard', placing Paul in Rome as these were the only serving soldiers allowed in Italy, namely the emperor's 13,000-strong elite bodyguard. If the letter was written elsewhere like Caesarea, it is suggested that they were the bodyguard of the local governor. Whoever they were, the good news of Christ had been heard close to the centre of power.

Chapter 2 In Philippians 2, verses 6-11, Paul is often thought to be quoting an early Christian hymn. Such means of bringing together key teaching were common in Paul's day. Acts 16:25 refers to Paul's use of these hymns while in the Philippian jail. If this was an early hymn then it would certainly be a good one to use at Philippi. There are a number of hymns based on this passage: e.g. 'At the name of Jesus', 'All praise to Christ' and 'Before the heaven and earth'.

Paul sees the Christian life and testimony as like stars in the sky. With all the lights that burn through the dark hours of today's world, it is only when we are in places far away from habitation that we can catch a glimpse of the night sky as those in Philippi would have experienced on a clear night. Thousands of extra stars appear amid the black background of space. We are called to be the light of the world, a light shining for Christ 'in the midst of a crooked and perverse generation' (2:15).

Sacrifices or libations to the gods (2:17-18) were the norm of Paul's day. Often wine was poured, but sometimes water. Paul thinks of his life as being poured out over the sacrifice of suffering for the gospel that they are making in Philippi. In the Old Testament, Numbers 15:3-10 sees the drink offering as adding completeness to the main offering. Paul sees it as a privilege to put the finishing touch to the work of the church there. He longs that the fruit of the gospel will be evident in the life of the church.

Paul is hoping to send Timothy and Epaphroditus to them to share their news. Even in these days of webcam and mobile communication, being with a loved one in the flesh is still something for which we long. How hard it must have been in those days when letters took months to arrive and the post was by no means reliable. It is much less than a century ago that international mail could arrive with some security. Many of the early 'airmail' flights never reached their destination and even today war and civil unrest can cause a breakdown in communication.

Messengers like Timothy (2:19) were seen as personal representatives and given equal honour. That practice exists today with ambassadors. Paul is hoping he can wait to send Timothy once there is news of the verdict in his trial. So he seems to have sent Epaphroditus with this letter. By the time this epistle is being read they will have rejoiced in his safe arrival, but Paul would have to wait a long while to know if the letter had even arrived. With virtually no medical facilities, as is still the case in many parts of the world, the people of Paul's day depended on prayer for healing. The pagans would use gods associated with healing, like Asclepius, and the major healing centre at Pergamum. Christians knew of the many healing miracles Christ had performed while on earth and continued to trust in him for healing. Illness, such as Epaphroditus had suffered before, was only part of the risk involved in bringing this letter to Philippi. It is probably just an interesting coincidence that gamblers invoked Venus, goddess of gambling, with the word *epaphroditus*. Paul certainly would not be thinking in such terms, although it may have been a word play that was meaningful to those of his day and the reason his messenger was given that name by his parents.

Chapter 3 We know that there were few Jews in Philippi, so this opposition to Paul's teaching may have come from visiting Jews, or even Christians who still refused to accept the ruling of Acts 15. Very few dogs were kept as pets. Most were used as guard dogs, or they were strays scavenging around the city. Signs with 'beware of dog' have been found in Roman cities. In many countries today dogs can be carrying rabies, so it is best to keep one's distance. Paul points out that he fully understands these teachings, having come out of strict Judaism. Now he regards 'everything as loss because of the surpassing value of knowing Christ Jesus my Lord'.

Paul knows he cannot give up and rest on his past record. So he uses the language of the athlete (3:12-16). Fit athletic bodies were highly prized in his day. Even small towns had a place set aside for exercise, often linked with the public baths. Competitions like the Olympic Games in southern Greece took place in most regions. So Paul has his eyes fixed firmly on the finishing line.

He is keen that these citizens of Rome, and others who had not attained such a status, should strive for the highest rank of all (3:20): citizenship of heaven. Roman citizenship may have protected Paul on his first visit and was enabling him to stand before the emperor's court. However, like his Jewish credentials, its worth was insignificant when compared to the glory of being a citizen of heaven.

Chapter 4 Scrolls varied in length. Paul is using size 2 for this letter. Books like Acts were written on size 4, Romans on size 3 and the letter to Philemon on size 1. So, as Paul notices he is running out of space, we now have a series of notes.

Euodia and Syntyche are Greek female names. As we know from Lydia, women could hold positions of considerable importance and there are inscriptions from Philippi showing that women held such positions in the city. Some maintain that Clement (v.3) was the same person as the one who wrote an early Christian letter from Rome to Corinth, but the name was fairly popular at that time and there is no indication from his letter that he is the same person.

Greek and Roman philosophers taught the importance of thinking and repeating lists of virtues (4:8-9). Muslims today have their 'wonderful names of Allah' on which they spend many hours in contemplation. Excellence (*arete*) was the key to Greek virtue.

Paul ends with a note of thankfulness and rejoicing. The philosophy of the day taught the need for gratitude. For Paul this was no philosophical concept – it was reality. Much of his mission seems to have depended, in an earthly sense, on the gifts of support that came from the Philippian church and he is very much aware of the sacrifice they had made for him in that way. In 4:18 Paul uses the word that was written on the receipts of his day: I have received – *dexamenos*. He wants to make it clear that everything is open and above board.

Thessalonica Acts 17:1-9

Paul and his companions arrived in Thessalonica from Philippi. That was a journey of about 100 miles along the Via Egnatia with night stops at the very least in Amphipolis and Apollonia. They probably decided not to stop in these places so as to put some distance between them and Philippi. They may also have discovered, when seeking a place to stay, if those in Philippi had not already told them, that there was no Jewish community with whom they could form a base.

Thessalonica, at the time, seems to have had a population of around 200,000, so it is no surprise that there was a Jewish community there. We do not know how long Paul stayed in Thessalonica but we have some clue from the mention by Paul that while he was there the church in Philippi sent him at least two donations towards his work (Phil. 4:16) and also that while in Thessalonica Paul supported himself through his tent-making: see 1 Thessalonians 2:9 and 2 Thessalonians 3:7-12. He may have been there for several months, so it is fairly certain that the three Sabbaths (Acts 17:2) refer to the start of his time there, when he was concentrating on bringing the gospel first to the Jews (Acts 13:46; Romans 1:16).

When evangelizing among the Jews, Paul continued his practice of using proof-texts from the Old Testament to show how Jesus fulfilled the predictions of the Messiah – his suffering, death and resurrection – just as Jesus had taught the disciples on the road to Emmaus (Luke 24:13). It was a mix of persuasion – he reasoned, explained and proved – and proclamation. Here, as elsewhere, we get the impression that Paul carefully set out the gospel and was open to careful examination as to the truth of his interpretation of the scriptures. It is not surprising that the Jews were jealous (v.5) when we read in verse 4 that a great many devout Greeks and not a few of the leading women turned to Christ. William Ramsey follows the Western text in claiming there were four groups among those converted – Jews, Greeks, God-fearers and well-known women. Along with Jason, Aristarchus and Secundus (Acts 20:4) may have been early followers. There is evidence from this time in Thessalonica that women held leadership roles, even as head of the synagogue.

Jason may well have been a Jew named Joshua who used an equivalent local name. He may have been a tent-maker used by Paul as his base, or an early follower who provided Paul and his companions with a place to stay. We have no mention of Paul staying in the inns, which had an unsavoury reputation. His normal practice was to stay with a local family.

Luke describes correctly the form of government that existed in Thessalonica. There was the assembly of the people (*demos*) which existed in the so called 'free cities', and the five or six *politarchs* or magistrates, an office peculiar to Macedonian cities.

We know from Suetonius that there had been problems around this time in Rome which had led to the Emperor Claudius expelling the Jews over one Chrestus, and the magistrates in Thessalonica might have suspected Paul was linked with these troublemakers (Acts 18:2). The charges were very serious: namely, disturbing the peace by bringing in an illegal religion (*religio illicita*) and proclaiming another king. We know from the letters to the Thessalonians that Paul had focused some of his teaching on the Second Coming, and any hint that he was proclaiming another king, now or in the future, would be seen as a challenge to the emperor and rule of law.

New cults were common in those days and we know Thessalonica was a centre for the Egyptian cults of Serapis and Isis, so it is unlikely that this was the first time the magistrates had had to deal with such problems. It may have been that Jason and the early followers second-guessed what was likely to happen and hid Paul until they could sort out the problem. In the circumstances the magistrates behaved very sympathetically. It is likely that the evidence was not strong and the man accused, Paul, could not be found, so the best way was to exile him from the city. Exile was a common punishment in Roman times. Jason was asked to give a security that Paul would not return. The Latin is *satis accipere* and the Greek *labontes to hikanon* is a direct translation. We do not know if this was a sum of money or some other security. Paul respected the ban put on his stay in Thessalonica and may have referred to it in 1 Thessalonians 2:17-18 where some maintain that Satan was a reference to the city authorities who were forbidding his return. In such circumstances the ban was usually lifted when the magistrates concerned left office. Paul seems to have visited again on his later journeys.

In conclusion, William Barclay comments on the phrase 'These people who have been turning the world upside down have come here'. He writes,

That was one of the greatest compliments which has ever been paid to Christianity. The Jews had not the slightest doubt that Christianity was a supremely *effective* thing. Further it is a challenge. T R Glover quoted with delight the saying of the child who remarked that the New Testament ended with *Revolutions.* When Christianity really goes into action it must cause a revolution both in the life of the individual and in the life of society. (*Acts of the Apostles*, Daily Study Bible, St Andrews Press 1953, p.139)

Letters to the Thessalonians

1 Thessalonians

Some Bible versions begin 1:1 with a greeting from Silvanus; other translations change his name back to the more familiar Silas. With Greek and Latin being the international languages and with numerous local languages like Hebrew, those who lived at this time often had various ways of writing their names. Perhaps the one we know best is the switch in Saul (Hebrew) to Paul (Greek) or Paulus (Latin). Maybe here Paul is stressing his and Silas' Roman citizenship.

He is writing to the church of the Thessalonians. The word *ekklesia* was the common word of the day for an assembly. Paul stresses that a Christian assembly is 'a community beloved and chosen by God in a past eternity, rooted in God and drawing its life from him, and exhibiting this life of God in a faith which works, a love which labours and hope which endures'. (John Stott, *Message of the Thessalonians*, IVP 1991, p.32)

1:6 'You became imitators of us and of the Lord'. The Greek philosophers made imitation of their lifestyle a key factor in training students. Paul urges imitation of God in Ephesians 5:1 and of his own example in 1 Corinthians 4:16. So although such a practice was the norm in the society of his day, we do not find mention of it very frequently in the New Testament.

1:8 'Your faith…known everywhere'. It is obvious that news did spread around in spite of the poor communication network of Paul's day. The New Testament only gives us a glimpse of the many Christians who were travelling around between the churches and passing on news in the process. This ease of communicating personal news did not really improve for another 1,800 years. It has now exploded with the use of the internet.

However, it is obvious that there were often long periods when news did not get through and that caused considerable anxiety as it has done down the centuries. Several times Paul stresses how difficult he found it being separated from those in Thessalonica. Sending Timothy (1 Thess. 3:2) only partly compensated for his forced exile. He is concerned that they are being persecuted (3:3-4) and how they will react to such trials. He prays constantly for them (3:10).

The beginning of chapter 2, where Paul recounts recent events, reminds us that his letter is firmly grounded in the situation that existed in his day. This was a common style of the day, grounding teaching in the experience of the reader. There were many wandering philosophers and religious gurus so it is no surprise that Paul seeks to show that he is one who is bringing the true gospel. In 2:13 Paul expresses his thanks that he was accepted as bringing the word of God. Stories abounded in all cultures of the day of those who had failed to recognize a true messenger and others who had accepted the teaching of a false messenger.

'We were gentle among you, like a mother caring for her little children' (2:7). Many Greek writers of the day extolled a mother's gentleness. However, where Roman influence dominated, a natural mother was often described as severe, and in the wealthier homes a baby was often handed over to a 'wet nurse' whose key characteristic should be gentleness. In such a situation it is no surprise that in Roman society many children grew up with a strong love for their 'wet nurse'. It is interesting that a man as tough physically and mentally as Paul – and we have ample evidence of this – should have described his ministry in this way.

When Paul refers to working 'night and day' he probably means that because part of his day, probably the long siesta time in the heat, was taken up with teaching, he continued working into the evening hours. Such work cannot have been easy with only the light from an oil lamp and so was certainly seen as 'going the second mile'.

The crown (2:19) probably refers to the victor's wreath or garland which was a common reward in Paul's time, rather than the royal crown reserved for God. In this instance Paul sees his crowning glory in the faithful perseverance of the Thessalonians.

Several passages in this letter deal with the end-times and what happens when we die. Jewish apocalyptic writers often taught of a time of suffering before the 'Day of the Lord', and Jesus had predicted that the preaching of the gospel would bring much suffering (e.g. Matthew 24). In 4:16 the Lord is pictured as coming back with a loud command and a trumpet call. Such means were the common way of giving orders in the battles of his time.

In chapter 4 Paul deals with the practical matter of sexual immorality. He may have heard of a specific issue in the church family or just be reflecting the culture of his day. Craig Keener comments, 'Unmarried Greek men (i.e. Greek men below the age of thirty) commonly indulged in intercourse with prostitutes, slaves and other males; Greek religion and culture did not provide any disincentive for doing so.' (Bible Background Commentary, 1993 p.590) Roman law only forbade such practice if it was between two people of the upper class. Jewish law was much stricter and only allowed for premarital sex between those who had already made a covenant to be married. The Jews therefore looked on all Gentiles as sexually immoral.

In 4:12 Paul urges Christians to work so that they are not dependent on others. This issue was to arise again in Corinth, from where he was probably writing this letter. Some criticized Paul for lowering his standing by being involved in manual work. Paul felt this was a better way than many travelling teachers of his day who sponged on those they taught.

In chapter 4 Paul refers to the *parousia* or coming of Christ. Walter Braur in his Greek-English lexicon comments:

> On the one hand, the word served as a cult expression for the coming of a hidden divinity, who makes his presence felt by a revelation of his power … On the other hand, *parousia* became the official term for a visit of a person of high rank, especially of kings and emperors visiting a province … These two technical expressions can approach each other closely in meaning… (*A Greek- English Lexicon of the New Testament* 5th edition 1958)

John Stott comments, 'Thus the coming of Jesus, Paul seems to be hinting by the mere adoption of this word, will be a revelation of God and a personal, powerful visitation by Jesus, the King.' (*Message of Thessalonians*, Bible Speaks Today 1991, p.97)

Although some main streets in the great cities like Antioch had street lighting, elsewhere the only light at night came from the moon and stars. It is not surprising that the night was (and in many places still is) the main opportunity for thieves, drunken parties and immorality (5:4-7). Paul, therefore urges Christians to be alert and self-controlled, living, whatever the time, as belonging to the day, self-controlled and putting on faith and love.

Paul stresses in 5:23 our wholeness of body, mind and spirit. By dividing soul from body some philosophers maintained that any physical act could not affect the soul. Others like Cicero divided the soul into two, and yet others like the

Stoics into eight compartments. Paul wants to stress that we are a unity of person and it is on this basis that we are judged.

As was the custom of the day, Paul was using an amanuensis to write his letter but in 5:25-8 he adds his personal greeting. John Stott comments, 'If a local church is to become a gospel church, it must not only receive the gospel and pass it on, but also embody it in a community life of mutual love. Nothing but the grace of Christ can accomplish this.' (ibid p.135)

2 Thessalonians

Paul's second letter, probably written in Corinth after receiving some more news of the church in Thessalonica, is aimed more towards the Jewish converts. In Chapter 1, when Paul responds to issues arising out of his teaching on the Second Coming, he does so against the background of Jewish thought of his day on such matters as rewards for the righteous and punishment for their persecutors. In 1:9 we have a quote from the Septuagint (a Greek translation of the Hebrew scriptures used extensively by Jews living outside Palestine).

It may have been that the Gentile converts had read too much of their cultural background into Paul's first letter. Greek philosophy taught of the escape of the soul, not a resurrection of both body and soul, so some may even have assumed that the end had already come and in some way they were living in a resurrected state. Teaching about being born again may have reinforced this view (2:2).

It is not easy to work out if Paul is referring to any particular person of his day when he refers to the 'secret power of lawlessness already at work' (2:6-12). We know that in his time there was an increasing emphasis on the deity of the emperor; indeed the previous Emperor Gaius Caligula, in AD 40 had tried to set up his statue for worship in the Jerusalem temple. Caligula had designated himself *theos epiphanous neos* (the new god revealed). The Syrian governor, realizing what would happen, took his time in enacting the order and was able to ignore it when Caligula was assassinated the following year. For the Jews this attempted action would certainly have fitted Paul's description here, and combined with Claudius exiling Jews from Rome, there may have been a general feeling, especially in the Jewish community, that these were the lawless end times. Emperor-worship already existed in Thessalonica. Archaeologists have uncovered a temple dedicated to the divine Julius and Augustus. Emperor-worship was seen as a reciprocal act. Rome gave the city many benefits, and in return the citizens invested in the imperial temple to show their loyalty and gratitude.

There has been a lot of speculation about to whom Paul was referring as the restrainer (2:7). Some have linked it with Claudius (his name comes from the Latin – to restrain) whose reign was better than that of Gaius or Nero who followed him, but this seems rather fanciful. Paul may just have been thinking of the way God was at work protecting his people. Whatever and whoever Paul refers to, his key point is that the end event has not yet come. The Day of the Lord, with all that it brings, is in the future.

The importance of passing on traditions (2:15) was very much part of Jewish and Greek culture. Each Greek family passed on its household gods and the ways of worship. Plato comments, 'The ancients, who were better than we and lived nearer the gods, handed down the tradition'. Jesus rebuked the Pharisees because they emphasized tradition above the scriptures (Mark 7:13). Here Paul is referring back to his teaching among them and to his first letter, neither of which were more than a few years earlier but were based on the teachings of the first apostles.

In 3:6 Paul deals with a problem of idlers. These may have been people who assumed the Day of the Lord had happened or would do so shortly, so there was no sense in working. They may have been those who felt manual work was below them and despised Paul's tent-making ministry.

Even to this day in many lands the men do very little work, leaving the running of the house and sometimes the smallholding to the wife. In Paul's day slave labour often meant that men had very little indeed to do beyond meeting up with other men in the agora and discussing the latest gossip. Paul urges all Christians to work. If they did not need the income themselves, then it certainly was needed by the Christian poor locally or in places like Jerusalem.

Some Christians had been excluded from their family and community and with it their employment but the problem here is with those who were unwilling to work. Maybe they set themselves up as teachers of the faith. The *Didache*, an early church teaching manual, gives the rule that if a traveller comes, the church may help him for a few days, 'and if he wishes to settle among you and has a skill, let him work for his bread'.

Beroea (Berea) Acts 17:10-15

Paul and his companions leave Thessalonica under cover of darkness for Beroea. Beroea is approximately 45 miles south-west of Thessalonica, so it is at least a two-day journey. Beroea is to the south of the Via Egnatia on higher ground overlooking the Aliakmonas river and the foothills of the Olympian range to the south but within striking distance of the main road leading to Athens.

It is interesting that when Cicero (106-43 BC) was in Macedonia he found a lot of hostility to Roman rule in Thessalonica and in a letter to Piso he pointed out that he would sometimes escape to Beroea as a quiet retreat 'off the beaten track'.

We know from inscriptions that the place was inhabited in the fourth century BC and that after the Battle of Pydna in 168 BC it was the first place to surrender to the Roman forces. Beroea seems to have had a fairly large population in Paul's time and was probably a centre for agricultural trade which attracted enough Jews to form a synagogue.

Luke highlights the way in which those in Beroea reacted to Paul's teaching. He points out that they were more noble (*eugenesteroi*) than those in Thessalonica. He probably felt that people in Thessalonica judged the message on political and cultural grounds rather than from the teaching of their scriptures. They did not restrict their study to the synagogue on the Sabbath but every day (17:11) they 'welcomed the message very eagerly and examined the scriptures' to see whether what Paul was preaching was based upon the Old Testament. John Stott points out that

> they combined receptivity with critical questioning. The verb for examine (*anakrino*) is used of judicial investigations, as of Herod examining Jesus, (Luke 22:14-15) the Sanhedrin, Peter and John (Acts 4:9) and Felix, Paul (Acts 24:8). It implies integrity and absence of bias. Ever since then, the adjective 'Berean' has been applied to people who study the Bible with impartiality and care.'
> (*Message of Acts*, Bible Speaks Today 1990, p.274)

We read that in Beroea many believed, especially Greek women and some men of high standing. The inference seems to be that some of these believers were not from among the 'God-fearers' but from the wider pagan community *(Hellenidon ... andron ouk oligoi)*. Was this success in reaching out to such people one of the reasons why Paul felt bold enough on arriving in Athens to go to the Greeks rather than seek out the Jews? One of these men might have been Pyrrhus, whose son Sopater travelled with Paul. Paul had passed through Beroea (Acts 20:2) and we presume at that time Sopater joined his group travelling south to Athens and Corinth, where he stayed with Paul for three months. Note how Luke, knowing the boundaries of the Roman provinces, separates Macedonia from Achaea. Paul was forced to change his travel plans and went back though Macedonia (Acts 20:4) and then on to Troas for his return journey to Jerusalem.

William Barclay remarks on the courage of Paul, who seems to have spent his Christian life being persecuted from one town to the next. He quotes David Livingstone, who when asked where he was prepared to go (he had originally planned to serve in China) replied: 'I am prepared to go anywhere, so long as it is forward.'

Luke's account does not fill in all the details about how Paul reached Athens. Jews from Thessalonica arrived, intent on catching Paul. Maybe they had the ear of the provincial authorities, because the church there decided he must leave that province for Achaea. It is not clear whether he travelled towards the coast and then, having given his persecutors the slip, took the road down to Athens, or whether he went to one of the small ports along that coast like Methone or Dium and then on by sea to Athens.

We are not totally certain how and when Silas and Timothy (v.15) linked up with Paul again. They seem to have come to Athens (1 Thess. 3:1), but then Timothy was sent back to Thessalonica (1 Thess. 3:2) and Silas possibly to Philippi (Acts 18:5) where he was able to collect further funding to support Paul's work (Phil. 4:15).

Athens Acts 17:15-34

Much has been written about whether Paul's visit to Athens was a success or a failure. Before looking at the events of Acts 17 in more detail it is helpful to bear in mind the following facts:

a) Athens in Paul's day had a population of less than 10,000 people. Historically it was a place of interest but for around 300 years it had been of little importance. Cities like Thessalonica and Corinth had around twenty times the population. They were the key places for Paul and the early church. So it is not surprising that in the early church we have mention of Corinth and Thessalonica in letters and visits, as well as representatives at the councils of the church, and no mention of Athens. In modern terms Athens would be a parish in the diocese of Corinth. Today the roles are once more reversed. Corinth is a small town and Athens the major city and capital of Greece.

b) Luke only gives an outline of three of Paul's sermons. In Acts 13:16-41 we have one preached to those who were Jews or well versed in the Old Testament. In Acts 14:15-17 we have a short address to illiterate pagans at Lystra. Here in Acts 17:22-31 we have a sermon or explanation of the faith, preached to those who had no knowledge at all of the Old Testament. It is very unlikely that Luke, who was writing in defence of Christianity, would use as one of his two sermon outlines, one that was regarded as a flop. Indeed Luke does not see it that way in that he points out some important people were converted and that Paul was invited to return and continue his teaching in front of the top people of the 'city'.

John Stott asks,

> What should be the reaction of a Christian who visits or lives in a city which is dominated by a non-Christian ideology or religion, a city which may be aesthetically magnificent and culturally sophisticated, but morally decadent and spiritually deceived or dead?' What Paul saw was a *kateidolos* 'a veritable forest of idols. (*Message of Acts*, BST, 1990, p.276-7).

As we look in more detail at the background to Athens in Paul's time it is worth keeping that question to apply to our own lives today.

To the people of Paul's day the fact that Athens was now just a small town did not affect its historical status as the place where Socrates, Plato and Aristotle taught and where the buildings reflected its former glory. Delphi, the site of the great oracle, was also a small town. So although some of the famous shrines of the ancient world, like the temple of Artemis in Ephesus, were in large cities, many of the centres of religion and philosophy were not.

It also helps to realize that for Paul the fine buildings of Athens were poor compared to the temple of Herod in Jerusalem or some of the civic buildings in Antioch. Antioch also had magnificent streets and many mod-cons like street lighting, tap water and central heating. For the history of Athens and a description of the buildings see pages 33-39.

M C Tenny in *New Testament Times* (Eerdmans 1965) assumes that Paul arrived by sea, landing at the port of Piraeus five miles to the south-west of Athens. In this case he would have walked along a walled road built five centuries before to link the two places. Tenny describes the scene thus:

> Approaching Athens from the west side, Paul would pass the Dipylon cemetery where were buried many of the famous citizens of Athens. The tombs, some of which are still standing, were ornately sculptured. Entering through the Dipylon gate on the west, he would proceed eastward past the Hephaestion Temple ... patron of the metalworkers whose quarter was adjacent to it. Known now as the Theseum, the Hephaestion is still standing, and is one of the best preserved temples of Greece. At the end of the avenue was the agora.

Paul, as usual, found the synagogue. It probably had a small membership but had attracted some 'God-fearers' from among the local population. We do not hear the result of this work.

Paul also made use of the opportunity that existed in Athens, probably more than any other place, of engaging the attention of people in the agora. This was the centre of life in Athens. On the western side, in the foothill of the Acropolis, were the main public buildings: the prytaneum containing the everlasting flame, the senate house (*bouleuterion*) and the temples of Apollo and Ares, behind which was the *metroon* or city record house. On the east side was the main commercial and shopping area. The whole area was filled with pillars mounted with gods, especially the god Hermes. The Parthenon dominated the skyline, as it still does, and in it was the huge gold and ivory statue of Athena, whose gleaming spear point was visible from up to forty miles away.

In the agora Paul soon found himself in dispute with followers of the two main schools of philosophy of his day. Epicurus (342-270 BC) claimed that real pleasure in this life was achieved by a peaceful life free from pain, desires, fear and any anxiety about death, which was the end of all life. For him the gods existed but they had no influence over humanity. Anything that happened was by chance and certainly not the action of the gods. He drew many followers from among the upper classes.

The Stoics were disciples of Zeno of Cyprus (340-265 BC). They took their name from the colonnade or stoa in Athens' agora where he had taught. He too emphasized the need to live in harmony with all, especially nature. This was pantheism with god as the world-soul. He emphasized rational thought and being self-sufficient. In that case everything was a matter of fate in the hands of the gods and we can do nothing to prevent it. (For a clear description of these two schools of philosophy see David Gooding, *True to the Faith,* Hodder 1990, pp.294-9.)

The Stoics saw themselves as guardians of the old traditions and their charge against Paul was couched in similar terms to the charge of impiety laid against Socrates. Socrates had been brought before the Areopagus and now Paul, the bringer of this new faith, had also to stand before them. Maybe Paul was thinking of Athens when he wrote in 1 Corinthians 1:20-21, 'Where is the wise man? Where is the scholar? Where is the philosopher of this age? Has not God made foolish the wisdom of the world? For since in the wisdom of God the world through its wisdom did not know him, God was pleased through the foolishness of what we preached to save those who believe.'

Paul is accused of being a babbler (*spermologos*) a word that comes from the sound of a flock of birds picking up fallen grain. It then meant someone going about picking up scraps of ideas and passing them on without knowing their true meaning, and eventually it was used of any charlatan. Those who heard him were certainly confused, assuming that he not only was teaching about the God

Jesus, but also another female goddess, Anastasis. If they were not concentrating on Paul's teaching, such confusion is not too much of a surprise as the word *anastasis* was the one used by Christians for the resurrection.

The Areopagus Council was originally based on a hill near the Areopagus. However, since the fifth century BC it had met at the north-west corner of the agora in the royal portico (stoa basileios) . Today the Areopagus is the Greek Supreme Court. In Paul's time its membership was made up of the city elders. They were usually retired civil administrators (*archons*) who had shown honesty in their tenure of office. They were charged with maintaining Athens' reputation as a place of learning. We do not know if those who brought Paul before them did so out of any malice, or that they were just interested to see how he could produce a defence before this august body.

William Ramsey, in *St Paul the Traveller and the Roman Citizen,* (Hodder 1896) comments: 'The scene described here seems to prove that the recognised lecturers could take a strange lecturer before the Areopagus, and require him to give an account of his teaching and pass a test as to its character.'

It seems that nothing much else happened in Athens beyond philosophical discussion (v.21). Its reputation for this is cited in various historical writers: for instance, Demosthenes pointed out that when threatened by Philip of Macedon the Athenians did nothing about defending the city and just kept talking.

Paul's defence Acts 17:22-31

Luke obviously gives us a précis of Paul's main points. He does not start from the Jewish scriptures but from where his hearers are. Paul pointed out, 'I have become all things to all men so that by all possible means I might save some' (1 Cor. 9: 20-22).

17:22-23 Xenophon described Athens as 'one massive altar, one great sacrifice where is it easier to find a god than a man'. Paul had noticed among these an altar to *agnosto theo* – the unknown god. We have evidence from the historians in the second and third century (Pausanias and Philostratus) that there were such altars, and indeed it would have been rather foolish for Paul to have based his opening gambit on something that was not known to his hearers. Some sources suggest that an outbreak of plague was stopped in Athens when, after sacrificing to the many known gods with no result, the Athenians had realized they did not know the name of the god who could help, so they sacrificed on a new altar that they erected 'to the unknown god'. A slightly different story is told by Diogenes in around AD 200. He claims that the reason for these altars was that the Athenians, at the time of the plague, let loose from the Areopagus a flock of black and white sheep. Wherever each lay down it was sacrificed to the nearest god; if one lay down elsewhere, an altar was dedicated to the unknown god and the sheep was sacrificed on it.

17:24-28 Paul focuses on the nature of God and our response to him. His key point is that God is the creator of everything and does not live in temples. Such teaching was not new. Paul would have known such verses from his own scriptures. Solomon had prayed in 2 Chronicles 6:18, 'Will God really dwell on earth with men? The heavens, even the highest heavens, cannot contain you. How much less this temple I have built.' He also knew that such teaching existed in Greek philosophy. In the fifth century BC Euripides had asked, 'What house built by craftsmen could enclose the divine form?'. Paul is teaching that God is *everywhere*, but not in the Stoic sense that god inhabits *everything*.

The Athenians boasted that the gods had made them a special people (*autochthonous*) and everyone else was inferior. Paul points out that everyone is equal before God and it is God who makes the key decisions, not men, as to where they should dwell.

Once more Paul grounds his argument by quoting from two of their pagan poets. Epimenides was a poet from Crete around 600 BC. Paul obviously had learnt of this work, maybe while studying in Tarsus, which in his day had a famous philosophy faculty. He quotes from the same poem again in Titus 1:12, 'Cretans are always liars, evil brutes, lazy gluttons'. Here Paul quotes from the following stanza,

> 'But you god are not dead; you live and abide for ever,
> For in you we live and move and have our being.'

His second quote is from a poet from his own home area of Cilicia. Three hundred years earlier Aratus had written:

> 'It is with Zeus that every one of us in every way has to do,
> For we are also his offspring'.

Paul is pointing out that even their own poets taught in a similar vein. He is not teaching something new but explaining clearly what was accepted teaching. C S C Williams in the *Acts of the Apostles* (A & C Black) comments, 'The remarkable thing about this famous speech is that for all its wealth of pagan illustration its message is simply the Galilean gospel, "The kingdom of God is at hand; repent and believe the tidings".'

It is important to note that Paul here differs from the Stoics. William Neil, in *The Acts of the Apostles,* New Century Bible Commentary (Eerdmans 1987), pp.191-2, comments,

> When Paul speaks of Christ living in us he is not reflecting the Stoic doctrine of the immanence of God. God is indeed in us as the Stoics said, but he is not identical with us or with the natural world, which was their claim. He is independent of man and nature and is the source of all life. ... However much Paul in his argument has sought to meet the philosophers on their own ground by using language and ideas that were common to both paganism and Christianity, he proceeds now to emphasize the difference.

One method of preaching is based on these Latin verbs *placere, docere, movere*. Paul had grabbed their attention and pleased them with his knowledge of their culture. He now teaches about Jesus before seeking to move them towards a decision. If his hearers had any delusion that Paul was accepting either polytheism or Stoic pantheism, he now clearly states in Acts 17:30 that God had overlooked the ignorance that had led to such false teaching but now, through his final and clear revelation in Christ, God expected a true response. Otherwise judgment would fall. The resurrection of Christ was proof that this was indeed the true message from God. It is obvious that Luke does not repeat this part of Paul's sermon as his readers would already know such facts.

Paul's teaching about the resurrection and judgment was certainly moving into a new radical doctrine. The Epicureans denied any immortality and most other Greek philosophers thought of any future existence as being in a shadowy world. Others, who followed Plato, took up a teaching similar to Buddhism where the enlightened soul could free itself from this world and be absorbed back into god.

Dr Loveday Alexander comments: 'It is noticeable, how closely the agenda of this speech follows the gospel that Paul himself claims to have preached to the Gentile converts of Thessalonica: see 1 Thessalonians 1:9.' (*Acts*, People's Bible Commentary, BRF 2006, p.137)

The response Acts 17:32-34 It is hard to judge what Paul felt about the effectiveness of such a meeting. He seems to have been much more comfortable putting across his message to the 'God-fearers' who were linked to the synagogues. Certainly he went on to Corinth determined to preach nothing among them but Christ crucified (1 Corinthians 1:20-25 and 2:1-6) and to denounce the 'wisdom of this age'. However, Paul in Athens, although he obtains the attention and some common thinking with his hearers, very soon moves into Christian teaching to which some sneered or mocked.

The important matter, as Luke stresses, is that some believed: including Dionysius, a member of the Areopagus, Damaris and a number of others. Eusebius claimed that Dionysius was the first bishop and martyr of Athens but we have no early evidence for this. How Damaris heard his message – she was obviously not a member of the council – we just do not know. Some commentators, following William Ramsey, think she was an interested bystander who may have been a mistress of one of the council members. It seems more likely that she was one of the 'god-fearers' who had heard Paul preach in the synagogue.

Corinth Acts 18:1-18

Corinth was built just south of the isthmus that connects the Peloponnese with the rest of Greece. Just north of the city was the route between the two ports of Cenchrea and Schoenus in the east and Lechaeum to the west. Some small boats were dragged across on rollers but in most cases goods were transhipped by porters. Today the Corinth canal serves the same purpose. To the south of the city was the Acropolis (1,886 ft) which not only provided a fortress but a place for pagan temples.

Corinth, like Thessalonica, had a population of around 200,000, which was twenty times the size of Athens. It fostered all the moral problems that exist in port cities and even from the fifth century BC the verb *korinthiazesthai* was used to describe sexual immorality. In the plays of the time, if a Corinthian was on the stage he was depicted as a drunk. (For a more detailed introduction to Corinth see pages 71-75)

Paul left the philosophical hotbed of Athens and set out west for the 50 miles to Corinth. On arrival he seems to have found a fellow tent-maker or leather worker (*skenopoios*) Aquila who, with his wife Priscilla, had recently moved to Corinth when the emperor Claudius had expelled the Jews from Rome. In a small place like Athens Paul may have found it hard to practise his trade so he would have been pleased that in Corinth he could continue to earn a living. The custom was that all Jewish rabbis were taught a trade. The saying was 'He who does not teach his son a trade teaches him to be a robber'. Tarsus, Paul's home town in Cilicia, was well known for a felted cloth made from goat's hair, known as *cilicium* and used for tents. In that case Paul would have been a weaver or tailor. However, the usual meaning of the word here is for someone who is a leather worker making tents and similar goods from animal skins.

It was usual, as it still is in many countries of the region, for those of a similar trade to work together. However, that was never an easy option for the Jews to work with those of other religions, as each trade had its patron god and there was a lot of pressure to attend the festivals linked to that god. For Paul to find another Jew in the same trade was a bonus. Paul in 1 Corinthians 9 points out that while in Corinth he supported himself by his trade. Some commentators suggest that Priscilla may have been a Jewish Roman citizen from the Prisca family (Paul uses that version of her name in his letters) who had married a Jewish freedman Aquila from Pontus (northern Turkey). From this follows a suggestion that they were fairly wealthy and had branches of their business in Rome, Ephesus and Corinth. Certainly Priscilla is often mentioned before her husband (Acts 18:18-19,26; Romans 16:3; 2 Timothy 4:19) which may indicate her higher status. Whatever their wealth or status, they became a vital part of the early church expansion. We do not know if they were already Christians when they came to Corinth. Suetonius says that Claudius 'expelled Jews from Rome because they were constantly causing riots in the cause of Chrestus'. That could be the earliest secular mention of Christianity. Certainly wherever Christ was preached among the Jews, riots seem to have ensued.

For a few weeks Paul, by earning his own income and no doubt teaching the faith to Priscilla and Aquila, was limited in further outreach to teaching in the synagogue every Sabbath. A stone fragment of the time found near the agora bears the inscription 'Synagogue of the Hebrews'. That could refer to the building that Paul used, but as stone was often reused, the location of such finds is insufficient evidence for the exact location of a building.

It appears that when Silas and Timothy arrived from Macedonia they brought with them some financial support so that Paul could devote himself exclusively to preaching the gospel (18:5). It was not long before the usual problems arose and Paul was no longer invited to teach in the synagogue. Along with financial help, Silas and Timothy brought good news of the churches in Macedonia. Paul had certainly been concerned about their welfare, having had to suddenly leave the three main centres of his work there. This news also encouraged Paul to devote himself to the task of bringing the gospel to the people of Corinth. This conviction that here was a place where God had called him to serve was confirmed (18:9) by a vision, with a message from God promising that he would not be harmed and that there were many people who were open to receive the gospel. So Paul stayed for what was for him a long period of eighteen months. He certainly needed this vision, as the pattern of his ministry since leaving Antioch (Acts 13) had been one of having to move on after only a few weeks, often under threat of his life. The cosmopolitan city of Corinth, with its great mix of peoples from many cultures following a wide variety of religions, helped to shield Paul from the Jewish opposition.

Paul is invited by Titius Justus to make use of his substantial house as a meeting place. Unfortunately his house was next door to the synagogue, which was not going to enamour his Jewish opponents. William Ramsey, whose books written at the turn of the twentieth century have had a considerable influence on commentators since, links Titius Justus with Gaius (Romans 16:23) of whom Paul writes: 'Gaius, whose hospitality I and the whole church here (Corinth) enjoy sends you his greetings'. In 1 Corinthians 1:14 Paul writes that he baptized Gaius along with Crispus the synagogue ruler. If Ramsey is right then it could be that Gaius was the *praenomen*, Titius the *nomen* and Justus the *cognomen*, so making the normal aristocratic Roman name of Gaius Titius Justus. Exactly when he came to Corinth is unknown but his family could have been among the Roman citizens settled there by Julius Caesar.

So not only is Paul teaching at an influential home next to the synagogue, but as an added thorn in the side of the Jews, Crispus and his family are also among his converts. Crispus was the ruler of the synagogue (*archisynagogos*). Paul baptized him and with him came his whole household. Already Stephanas and his family had accepted Christ (1 Cor.16:15) so these three important families would have provided a considerable number of followers and to them were to be added many other Corinthians (Acts 18:10). We can assume there were well over one hundred Christians worshipping in the home of Titius.

This must have been a massive encouragement to Paul, being able to settle into a long-term ministry with a large number coming to faith in Christ. His whole Christian life from the time he had to flee Damascus, when he was let down one night over the city wall in a basket, seems to have been one of persecution and danger. Here at last God had given him an open door.

It is no surprise to find that this peace did not last for long. Acts 18:12-17 tells of a serious attempt by the Jews to stop his ministry. It is July AD 51. A new proconsul has arrived in time for Corinth to host the Pan-Hellenic games that year. Achaea was ruled by a Senate appointee from 27 BC to AD 15. It then reverted to an appointment by the emperor (as Macedonia) until it was returned to the senate in AD 44. Gallio, or to give him his birth name Marcus Annaeus Novatus, the son of Marcus Annaeus Seneca, a distinguished orator from Spain, was the younger brother of Lucius Annaeus Seneca, a well known Stoic philosopher, dramatist and politician who remarked of him, 'No human is so pleasant to any person as Gallio is to everyone'. On the death of his father, Gallio was adopted by Lucius Junius Gallio and took on the name of his adoptive father. Ill health forced Gallio to retire early from office and under Nero he was killed, along with his other brother Mela (the father of the poet Lucan). His older brother Seneca was forced to commit suicide.

So working on the usual dating for Paul's ministry, this episode with Gallio occurred about halfway through Paul's time in Corinth. He is taken to the bema – a platform used for official pronouncements and judgments. One of the more interesting archaeological finds at Corinth has been this actual bema. The Jews brought the usual charge against Paul that he was promoting a *religio illicita*. Gallio took the line that this was really about an internal dispute within Judaism and it was not his role to judge such matters.

The judgment was very important at this time in the early church. It meant that for a considerable time Christianity was seen by the Roman rulers as a sect within Judaism, not an illegal religion. Up to this stage there had been no official judgment as to the status of the Christian church. The decisions of local magistrates, as in Thessalonica, would not have had any force outside their district. Now that an eminent proconsul had made a decision, other Roman rulers would follow this ruling. Later it gave Paul the confidence to appeal to Caesar.

Sosthenes, who had replaced Crispus as the synagogue ruler, is beaten up. Anti-Semitism was always near to the surface. They knew the Jews were not in favour with the emperor as he had recently expelled them from Rome, so now was a good opportunity to show their distaste of a group who were disliked for the special privileges they claimed and their business dealings. Gallio did not make any effort to stop this mob justice. It is always risky to link people of the same name but it is interesting that when Paul writes to the Corinthians (1 Cor. 1:1) he does so through Sosthenes. Did yet another ruler of the synagogue convert to Christianity?

So (18:18) Paul was able to continue his ministry before leaving in the spring of AD 52 to travel to Jerusalem, after first having a haircut at the port of Cenchrea. Such facts of day-to-day life are rarely mentioned but in this case it is linked into a vow, and Luke is making the point that Paul still retained some of the customs of Judaism. Some speculate that this hair cutting was at the start of a vow; others think that when Paul came to Corinth he made a Nazarite vow that he would not cut his hair until he had seen God's blessing and was now taking his cut hair to Jerusalem to offer up his vow on the altar.

We do not know what happened to Silas and Timothy but we do know that Aquila and Priscilla went with Paul as far as Ephesus, where they stayed for some time, possibly for about four years, leading a congregation in their home.

Letters to the Corinthians

1:2 Christians had no separate church buildings until the time of Constantine. This meant that most meetings were in the homes of the wealthier members who had big enough homes or courtyards. The shops in the market usually had an upper storey used as living quarters. The room, mainly unfurnished, would not hold more than about twenty people. The majority of homes were even smaller, as most activity took place outside and the home was only used for sleeping, as it is in many tropical lands today – so it was only the very rich who would have had a place large enough for the congregation to meet. When more than one home was used, then the tendency for division was even greater. Paul urges unity and asks (1:13), 'Is Christ divided?' Such a challenge to retain the unity of believers is still with us.

1:11 News had reached Paul by the usual route of travelling members. In this case it came through Chloe, who had various employees travelling between the two major ports of Ephesus and Corinth (Chloe could have lived in either city and was probably a wealthy businesswoman like Lydia of Philippi). Such message-carrying still exists in parts of the world, especially where the church is being persecuted.

1:12 In Corinth there was conflict, with church members forming groups behind their favourite teacher. Those of higher social status preferred Apollos with his fine rhetoric; those from an artisan background preferred Paul, who worked alongside them. Even today Christians align themselves with the denomination or the person who brought them to faith. Paul himself refers to the Jewish custom of being a disciple of a rabbi, in his case it was Gamaliel (Acts 22:3). Those from a pagan background in Corinth may have followed various philosophers. Paul longs that Christians will see themselves as followers of Christ, children of one heavenly Father.

1:14 Jesus had ordered his disciples to use baptism as an outward and visible sign of entry into the church just as the Jews had used the baptism of gentiles into Judaism. Whenever Matthew 28:19 was written down, it is obvious from the accounts in Acts and other writings that baptism and the Lord's Supper were adopted by the first disciples as normal practice.

1:18-25 The Greek love of rhetoric and philosophy could easily have led to those in the early church following teachers because of how they put across their message. It can still happen, but at least today we have the Bible and doctrines of the church like the creed as a means of testing such teachers. That was not the case in Paul's day, so it was vital for him to encourage Christians to stick to the basics, of which the death of Christ on the cross for us was paramount.

Going to the theatre for a play was common and one of the popular characters in the plays was rather like Shakespeare's fool, who appeared to be stupid but turned out to be the only one with a true message. Paul uses the picture of Christ's crucifixion in this setting, rather than the concept of the stone the builders rejected (Mark 12:10) which Jesus and the disciples used for those with a Jewish background.

So Paul stresses also that Christians are made wise in Christ. In society status depended very much on one's parents. Paul himself could claim to have been born a Roman citizen (Acts 22:28). Now, through new birth in Christ, all Christians were of equal status before God and should treat each other in that way as brothers and sisters.

When writing to the church in Rome from Corinth, Paul mentions that Erastus the city treasurer (Romans 16:23, Acts 19:22 and 2 Timothy 4:20) was one of the church members. Various inscriptions have been found at Corinth which refer to him. About five years before Paul came to Corinth, a 14,000-seat theatre had been renovated and a large stone plaza laid at the north-east corner. An inscription found there reads, 'Erastus in return for his aedileship laid (this area) at his own expense'. The *aedile* was originally someone appointed to oversee the municipal buildings but later took on other duties such as 'city treasurer'. Paul's comment that not many were influential or of noble birth reminds us of the many in that church whose name will never be found by the archaeologists.

4:1-2 Business owners often entrusted day to day transactions to freedmen and even slaves. Some had great influence and honour in society. It was vital that they were trustworthy and faithful.

4:9 Paul may be drawing this illustration from the games in the amphitheatres, when at the start of the proceedings the gladiators were shown to the crowd, followed by those condemned to fight with the wild beasts. *Te morituri salutamus* (We who are about to die salute you). However, it is important to note that such events were not common in the time of Paul. After years of research it has still not been shown that more than a handful of Christians ever suffered such a fate.

4:13 Philosophers often regarded the hoi polloi as refuse or trash. It appears that this sentiment was reversed, and often the people regarded the wandering philosophers, who depended on begging for their keep, in that light.

4:15 Paul refers to the practice of parents appointing a *paidagogos* who would look after a child on the way to and from school, teach him good manners and encourage him to learn. Modern translations use the term 'guardian'. Normally the *paidagogos* was a slave and so no substitute for a 'father', the position Paul claims as the one who brought them to Christ.

5 Any sexual act or marriage between a brother and sister was banned except in Egypt. In Paul's time those who sought to libel the emperor accused him of such scandals. Incest, including that with step-parents, in Roman law was punished by banishment. The synagogues also used the punishment of excommunication and banishment from the community for such sins. So Paul urges the church to 'Expel the wicked man from among you.'

6 The reference to courts may have arisen out of cases relating to chapter 5 but Paul broadens that to any law case. The synagogue had been the place for settling disputes among the Jews. Now that the church was drawn from many races and nationalities, the Christians were not sure where they should turn to settle disputes between themselves. So Paul urges that they form a Christian court similar to the one in the synagogue. The secular courts always showed favour according to social status. Paul could claim preferential treatment as a Roman citizen who topped such a list, with slaves coming at the bottom.

6:9-11 Corinth was renowned for its corrupt morality. The Acropolis housed the temple of Aphrodite. According to Strabo it had one thousand priestesses or sacred prostitutes, male and female, who came down each evening to ply their trade. 'Not every man can afford a journey to Corinth' was a much quoted proverb. Most inns were well stocked with prostitutes and that is why we do not read of Christians staying in such places. Sexual relations outside marriage were very common. Some philosophers advocated it and even indulged in public. They treated having sex on a par with the body's need for food. Many men did not marry until in their thirties and were usually sexually active well before that time. Because of the restrictions brought about through social status and slavery, many people never had the opportunity to marry. There was always a ready supply of prostitutes raised from the abandoned children of slaves. Dio Chrysostom is the only known pagan author to attack brothels on moral grounds. The Christian teaching of the 'body as the temple of the Holy Spirit' and 'honouring or glorifying God with your body' (6:19-20) was contrary to much pagan philosophy of the time.

Paul not only strongly condemns the sexual sins in verse 9 but also in verse 10 includes theft, greed, drunkenness, slander and swindling. Although some Corinthian Christians had been involved in such behaviour they were now washed, sanctified and justified.

Most versions of the Bible put comments like 6:12 in inverted commas: 'Everything is permissible for me' or 'I can get away with anything' as Paul quoting some of the slogans used by those in Corinth. In many places it is hard to work out when Paul is quoting and when he is being ironic. Such quotes or irony cannot be applied to Paul's condemnation of such immoral behaviour.

In Chapter 7 Paul now tackles the issue as to whether or not one should be married. Although there were some like the Essenes who practised celibacy, such a choice was not common in Paul's time. Some philosophers taught that a wise man should never be tied to marriage but should not inhibit his sexual desires. Paul teaches that marriage is the only place in which sexual relationships should take place and partners should not deny each other their conjugal rights.

7:12-16 Divorce was fairly common. Under Roman law either party could initiate it; under Jewish law only the husband could do so. Paul urges Christians thinking towards divorce to follow the teaching of Christ, although he realizes that in a situation where many of the members had become Christians after marriage, some would be driven from their homes. In Roman law the father kept the children, so a Christian mother by leaving her husband would lose the right to influence her children for Christ.

7:18 Exercise in the gymnasium and bathing took place in the nude and some Jews were having an operation to try and conceal their circumcision.

7:21 In Paul's day any slave revolt had led to many slaves being executed. Paul has to give advice from within the circumstances of the day. However, it is obvious from his writings that he regards all people as equal before God. A greater responsibility lies with Christians who lived in an age when the church had the power to bring about emancipation.

7:22 'A freedman when called is Christ's slave'. This refers to the fact that, although a master had freed a slave, a freedman still had some obligations to promote his master's interests, and for his part the master still accepted the freedman as part of his household. Freedmen also often adopted a name from their former master.

7:26f There does not seem to have been a move towards celibacy in the early church. Paul is basically only encouraging it for those like himself who are in the front line of service. However, Greek philosophers of all schools did encourage their followers not to marry. That was not the same as being celibate. Epictetus, the stoic, never married. He felt his teaching was of more value than producing children. He asked, 'How can one whose function is to teach be expected to run for something in which to heat the water to give the baby a bath?'

8:1-13 Food offered to idols (see also 10:18-33). Trade guild meetings were a vital part of commercial life, and tradespersons depended on such guilds for the right to practise their trade. Meetings were usually held in the temple of their patron god. Most people took the attitude of Socrates that sacrifices were a means of obtaining favours from the gods. At this time it was still possible to absent oneself from such meetings or to abstain from eating from the sacrificial meal. Later, sacrifice to the emperor became compulsory and led to many martyrs in the early church.

Paul points out that although he, and maybe those Christians partaking in these temple meetings, knew that the pagan gods were powerless, consideration had to be given to the impression such eating would give to others. However, when it came to meat sold in the market it was not up to the Christian to make detailed enquiry as to its source. In cities with a large Jewish population there were kosher markets, so probably those from a Jewish background continued to use their own supply. The poor probably did not eat meat very often and slaves depended on what they were given by their masters, so Paul is writing for the wealthier members of the church from a non-Jewish background.

Paul continues with his teaching about eating in Chapter 10 but before that he deals with his own position.

9:5 He points out that other Christian workers like Peter and James took their wives with them. It seems that when Jesus was at work during his life on earth the wives of the twelve apostles stayed at home. Now that overseas work involved a long period away from home, it appears that some were taking their wives along with them. We have no record of any of Paul's companions being accompanied by their wives, so was this a rule that he and Barnabas developed because they felt their journeys were too difficult? It would be surprising if none of them were married. Does the phrase 'to take a believing wife along with us' hint that some, and possibly Paul, were married but their wives did not believe. Many think that the status Paul had before his conversion implies that he was married, but his wife either refused to believe or was even taken away from him by her relatives. Records show that, in the secular world, if their position allowed, some officials took their wives with them but for those in the army and certain other jobs there was a ban on such travel.

9:6ff Paul is making it clear that he regards it as a 'right' of a full-time Christian worker to receive support and not have to engage in other work like his tent-making. However, in these circumstances at Corinth he does not feel it appropriate. As with so much of Paul's correspondence, we can only read between the lines and assume there were some special circumstances that caused Paul to work at Corinth. Acts 18:5 points out that Paul only seems to have worked while he was waiting for funds to arrive from Philippi. If that is the case, it does seem strange this was such a big issue. Paul certainly feels that those in Corinth – and there were obviously some wealthy members – were not pulling their weight in contributing to the Christian cause (see 16:1-4 and 2 Cor. 8-9).

9:24ff Corinth hosted the Isthmian games for the whole of Greece every two years. Their status was similar to those at Olympia which were held every four years. At Corinth the winner was awarded with a garland made from pine; at Olympia it was made from olive leaves. Boxers wore fingerless leather gloves up to the elbow. It was a very violent sport and in order to train for it a boxer had to have a sparing partner who would cause pain. Shadow boxing was not an adequate training method (9:26-27). So Paul is not running aimlessly or just beating at the air: his Christian discipleship involved real commitment and physical pain (see 2 Cor. 11).

10 Paul returns to where he left his argument in chapter 8 and now writes especially for those with a background in Judaism. We can assume that the events of the Exodus were so much part of Jewish history that the 'God-fearers' would also know about them. The events to which Paul refers are recorded in Exodus 32:4ff, the golden calf; Numbers 25, the Israelites have sex with Moabite cult prostitutes; and Numbers 21:5ff, poisonous snakes.

10:3 Paul uses a litotes when he writes that God was not pleased with most of them, for only Joshua and Caleb reached the promised land. This is a major warning to those at Corinth who were behaving like the Israelites by trusting in the Christian sacraments of baptism and eucharist, just as the Israelites had trusted in God's redemptive signs recorded in Exodus, like the passage through the 'sea' and the food from heaven but were severely judged.

10:14 Here and in 11:17-end we have the earliest reference to the eucharist and re-enactment of the Last Supper. Most pagan cults practised some form of meal in the presence of the gods, where wine was often used, but here Paul is obviously referring to the events in the upper room and, with them, to the Jewish Passover. In both instances the priests had their share of the offering and the people ate the rest of the sacrifice. Sharing a meal together was, and still is, seen as a sign of deep fellowship.

In 10:24 to 11:16 Paul deals with various cultural issues of his day, making the key point in verses 31 and 32: 'whatever you do, do it all for the glory of God. Do not cause anyone to stumble.'

An instance of this was whether a woman should cover her hair. The basic teaching of the day was that god or nature had created women to grow long hair and men to grow facial hair, so most allowed 'nature to run its course'. The wealthy women had elaborate hair arrangements and were keen for everyone to see their latest style; the poor followed the traditional custom of covering their heads. So to cover or not to cover was a class issue. There was also religious practice which applied to either sex where the Romans uncovered their heads and the Greeks covered their heads for worship. Certainly those who objected to women arriving with elaborate hairstyles were right in pointing out that they were distracting church members from concentrating on the worship of God and on being the family of Christ. So it appears that Paul finds various reasons to encourage all females to cover their heads. He follows a line also taught by the philosophical school called the Skeptics: 'that's the way it is'.

11:17-34 reveals one of the disadvantages of meeting in the homes of the wealthy Christians. The owner of the home would recline with his social friends in the dining room (triclinium) while others gathered in the courtyard (atrium). As the early celebrations of the eucharist or Lord's Supper were often incorporated into a meal, it added to the feelings of class division when the select few, usually men, were eating the best food and drinking the best wine in comfort while others even received nothing at all. James in his letter (chapter 2:1-4) also mentions this problem which existed in these house churches. It is no surprise that the church soon divorced worship from a meal and it has only been possible in a few wealthy areas of the world for this link to be re-established in recent years. In the same way it has taken many years for churches to claim that all seats are available, yet many visitors to a church, even today, soon discover that may still not be the case.

In chapter 12 onwards, Paul is able to point out that Christians from whatever background are accepted and gifted by God. Here the Holy Spirit is the great leveller. Paul has a random list of the Spirit's gifts to emphasize that all are equal and all are there to contribute to the church body. The picture of the body is not used in the Stoic sense of the head controlling the uneducated masses but to teach that all are equal in God's sight and all have their part to play.

There is a problem with certain gifts, especially those involving ecstasy. At the Greek oracular shrines, like Delphi, there were prophets who threw themselves into a state of ecstasy. Paul is concerned that the behaviour of some members might be seen as being possessed in an unhelpful way. In chapter 14 he refers to speaking in tongues. In Acts 2 the sign of the coming of the Holy Spirit was seen in God breaking the curse of Babel and enabling all those present to hear the gospel in their own tongue. Such a gift of the Spirit is still vital in places where there are many languages: for instance, the island of New Guinea is said to have over 1,000 distinct languages. Paul points out that if people cannot understand what is being said, they are in the position of those who were under judgment or, as Christ put it, they could hear but never understand. Paul is keen that if tongues are used they do not detract from the ability of all to join in the worship and understand what is being said (14:1-28). Perhaps his most telling phrase is in 14:19: 'But in the church I would rather speak five intelligible words to instruct others than ten thousand words in a tongue' (10,000 is the largest Greek number). One of the major blessings God had given the early church was that nearly all those with whom the early missionaries came into contact spoke Greek. There had been a major problem at Lystra (Acts 14:8) when a local language had been used, but the general rule was that, although people loved to hear the good news in their local language as in Acts 2, Greek was understood throughout the Roman empire. Those who did not speak Greek were regarded by the Greeks as barbarians (their words were no better than someone saying 'baa baa' like a sheep). Christians could feel they were part of one family because whatever their social status they spoke the same language.

In the interlude (chapter 13) Paul has emphasized that the key gift of the Spirit is love. As these comments are focusing on the background to the teaching, there is one major item to mention here, namely, Corinthian bronze (13:1). Corinthian bronze was highly prized but by Paul's time manufacture had dwindled and a lot of the trade was in second-hand items. This high-grade bronze was used to make sounding-boards (probably better than 'gong') which enabled orators to be heard in large gatherings like the theatre. In 13:12 finely polished bronze is used as a mirror, but even the best Corinthian bronze gave a very poor image.

Paul main emphasis in chapter 15 is that the resurrection is based on historical fact and he is able to cite hundreds of living witnesses to that fact. There were plenty of visions and secret communications which formed the basis of the other religions. Paul stresses that his message is based firmly on verifiable facts.

In Paul's day there were three basic teachings about the afterlife.

The Epicureans and Sadducees denied any afterlife. Herodotus tells of an Egyptian custom at a banquet of carrying round a coffin containing a wooden corpse with the message, 'Gaze here, and drink and be merry, for when you die, such will you be'. Catullus wrote, 'Let us live, my Lesbia, and let us love ... suns can set and then return again, but for us, when once our brief light sets, there is but one perpetual night.'

Many others accepted the immortality of the soul. For the Greeks this meant the obliteration of the body. Seneca wrote, ' I am a higher being and born for higher things than to be the slave of my body which I look upon as only a shackle put upon my freedom ... in so detestable a place dwells the free soul.' Plato taught that the body is the antithesis of the soul, as the source of all weaknesses, as opposed to what alone is capable of independence and goodness. Paul here and in 2 Corinthians 5:1-10 gives the Christian teaching that, although our present body is weak, 'one day we will be clothed with our heavenly dwelling'.

The Pharisees, and with them most Jews, looked towards the resurrection of the body. Paul points out that the clear evidence from the resurrection of Christ is that there is a resurrection body. Such a body is not the same as an earthly one but one of substance. Individuality will survive: I will still be me. There is a unity of body, mind and spirit. Christ showed by his incarnation that the body was not evil.

Much has been speculated about what Paul means in 15:29 by 'baptized for the dead'. In has taken a lot of deep digging to produce some explanation from the practices of his time. It is best to say that we just do not know.

In 15:32 Paul mentions, 'I fought wild beasts at Ephesus'. It is exceptionally unlikely that Paul, a Roman citizen, would have been in an arena with such animals and we have very little evidence anyway of their use. Certainly the theatre at Ephesus is of a design that if a wild beast entered there was no protection for the spectators nor enough room for any chase to take place. So the likely explanation is that Paul is speaking figuratively. St Ignatius (d.110) wrote, 'From Syria to Rome, by land and by sea, night and day, I am fighting with wild beasts. I mean these soldiers, to whom I am bound, for they are like ten leopards.' (Letter of Ignatius *To the Romans* 5:1).

In 15:32 Paul quotes from the Epicureans, 'Let us eat and drink, for tomorrow we die'. In 15:33 he quotes a popular saying of Menander, 'Bad company corrupts good character'. Although Paul does not base his doctrine on such statements he is happy to use them to ground his teaching into the culture of his day.

16:1 is evidence that by Paul's time, Christians had started making Sunday the normal day for worship in celebration of the resurrection.

16:3-4 The Jews living abroad sent vast sums of money to Jerusalem each year for the very high costs involved in the upkeep of Herod's magnificent temple. We know that the Jews in the much smaller town of Laodicea were sending an annual gift or levy of ten kilos of gold. Christians seem to have followed their practice but used the funds to assist the Christian poor. Both Jews and Christians sent their funds in a standard way through trusted representatives.

16:5-9 Travel was limited by the seasons, although it was possible to reach Corinth from Ephesus mainly by land, making a short sea crossing, possibly from Troas to Neapolis.

Paul concludes his letter by sending greetings, as was his common practice, dictated to his scribe with his own signature and personal note (16:21-24).

2 Corinthians

There is a difference of opinion among commentators as to whether this is one letter, or a compilation from Paul's other three letters to Corinth. As we are only dealing with the background here, it is not a matter for discussion. Much of the background has already been covered in the comments concerning 1 Corinthians but there are some distinctive aspects which need attention.

1:22 The Spirit is a seal. The custom was to seal letters with sealing wax. A scroll would be tightly wound and then tied with string or such substance before the seal of wax was placed on the knot and impressed by a signet ring or some other stamp, to show that no tampering had taken place – a custom that continued even in Britain until about fifty years ago. Such seals were also put on important goods, like seals on the wine amphoras. The Spirit is also an *arrabon* or deposit. Corinth was a major trading centre and it was common for merchants to make a down payment to a shipowner from whom they would purchase the goods on arrival. The term was used about deposits made to tradesmen for furniture and even to actors and dancers in advance of their performance. It was also used as a pledge of marriage rather like an engagement ring. So everyone in Corinth would understand Paul when he points out that the Holy Spirit living in us is a clear commitment by God to our future glory.

2:5 Under Greek and Roman law, once a person had served his punishment he was readmitted into the community. Paul urges this reinstatement for the man who had sinned. He was probably the one mentioned in 1 Corinthians 5:1-5.

2:14-17 W Barclay comments:

> In Paul's mind there is the picture of a Roman triumph and of Christ as a universal conqueror. The highest honour which could be given to a victorious Roman general was a Triumph. Before he could win it he must satisfy certain conditions. He must have been the actual commander-in-chief in the field. The campaign must have been completely finished, the region pacified and the victorious troops brought home. Five thousand of the enemy at least must have fallen in one engagement; a positive extension of territory must have been gained and not merely a disaster retrieved or an attack repelled. And the victory must have been won over a foreign foe and not in a civil war.

> In an actual Triumph the procession of the victorious general marched through the streets of Rome to the Capitol in the following order. First, there came the state officials and the

senate. Then there came the trumpeters. Then there were carried the spoils taken from the conquered land. For instance, when Titus conquered Jerusalem the seven-branched candlestick, the golden table of the shew-bread and the golden trumpets were carried through the streets of Rome. Then there came pictures of the conquered land and models of conquered citadels and ships. There followed the white bull for the sacrifice which would be made. Then there walked the wretched captives, the enemy princes, leaders and generals in chains, shortly to be flung into prison and in all probability almost immediately to be executed. Then there came the lictors bearing their rods, followed by the musicians with their lyres. Then there came the priests swinging their censers with the sweet-smelling incense burning in them. And then there came the general himself. He stood in a chariot drawn by four horses. He was clad in a purple tunic embroidered with golden palm leaves, and over it a purple toga marked out with golden stars. In his hand he held an ivory sceptre with the Roman eagle at the top of it, and over his head a slave held the crown of Jupiter. After him there rode his family, and finally there came the army wearing all their decorations and shouting Io triumphe! their cry of triumph. As the procession moved through the streets, all decorated and garlanded, amid the shouting, cheering crowds, it was a tremendous day, a day which might happen only once in a lifetime. That is the picture that is in Paul's mind. He sees the conquering Christ marching in triumph throughout the world, and himself Paul in that conquering train. It is a triumph which, Paul is certain, nothing can stop. (*The Letters to the Corinthians*, Daily Study Bible, St Andrew Press 1954, pp. 204-5)

By Paul's time such triumphs were only allowed for the emperor, and his dress and the symbols of Jupiter were there to reinforce his divinity.

K L Schmidt has speculated that Mark's account of the passion also picks up this idea of the Roman triumph with the purple robe, crown and staff, and the crucifixion. 'Mark is presenting an anti-triumph in reaction to the contemporary offensive self-divinization efforts of Gaius and especially Nero'. The purpose of such a portrayal is clear: one of the same Roman soldiers who first mocked

Jesus as a triumphant king is the one who joins God himself in confessing Jesus' lordship.

3:1-6 It was common practice in the Greco-Roman world for important patrons to write 'letters of recommendation' for travellers. The Jews made a point of doing this as there were very few public places of good repute to stay when on a journey. Consequently the vast majority of travellers sought out a place to stay among their contacts. Some abused this practice by forging such letters. Others did not favour the practice, so when Diogenes, a philosopher, was asked for such a letter, he replied, 'That you are a man is obvious to all; but whether you are a good or bad man your host will discover if he has the skill to distinguish between good and bad and if he is without that skill he will not discover the facts even though I write to him thousands of times.'

3:18 In Paul's time there was a movement towards the deification of the emperor. Roman emperors in their lifetime claimed to be turning into gods. Such teaching had been common in the east long before it was adopted by Rome and so gained ground there much earlier than in the west. It had begun with Augustus using this concept from the east as a means of encouraging loyalty. So the cult of Augustus et Roma became an expression of that. Nicolaus of Damascus observed, 'People gave him the name Augustus in view of his claim to honour; … and they revere him by building temples and by sacrificing to him, thus requiting him for his great virtue and acts of kindness towards them. By the time Paul began his missionary journeys there was considerable pressure from Rome for each town to promote the imperial cult.

4:7 Earthen or clay jars were plentiful, easily made and just as easily broken. An invading army would make the point of smashing jars used to store oil, wine and food as a means of ruining their defeated foe. In days before banks, even more precious treasure was sometimes hidden in such jars under a layer of corn or some other relatively low value substance.

5:10 We must all appear before the judgment seat (bema). Paul had been brought before such a seat. In some cases there was a panel of judges or a jury. So that no one would know the way jurors voted, each person was given two items. In Athens they were two bronze disks. One was solid, the other had a hole in the centre. When the time came to cast their votes they would put the disk which indicated their verdict into one jar and discard the other one into another jar.

The disks in the first jar would then be counted and the judgment announced on a majority verdict. No one saw into which jar the juror placed his disks.

5:20 In Paul's time ambassadors were usually the emperor's legates. In previous generations they had been messengers of the senate or other rulers. A legate was sent by the emperor to make it clear to rebellious places that they could expect the full force of the emperor's power against them if they did not sue for peace. Paul, as Christ's ambassador, urges the Corinthians to make their peace, be reconciled, with God. As the Corinthians were in a state of strife with Paul, Paul urges them to realize that behaving in this way towards Christ's ambassador was tantamount to being in a hostile state towards God.

6:14 Corinth, like all places at the time, had many temples where the gods were claimed to dwell. To show disrespect for the temple was to show disrespect for the god who dwelt in it. Many early Christians lost their livelihood because they would not compromise their faith by taking part in pagan ceremonies. Even if one could avoid these events in the temples, how could a Christian stonemason earn a living if he refused to build pagan temples or how could a Christian serve as a soldier when he had to sacrifice to the emperor. The issue for those in the early church, as it is for us today, is that as God lives in a Christian, so a Christian must keep his body pure and undefiled.

In Chapters 8-9 Paul is stressing that Christians give voluntarily. In the world of his day many rich members of society were relied upon to fund civic facilities. This was seen as a way of self-aggrandisement. Others were ruined by being forced into giving large sums towards these public works. Paul does not want Christian giving to come out of either of these situations.

9:8 Paul uses a favourite word for the Stoics, *autarkeia,* which means a life that is not directed to gaining possessions. It describes someone who is content with what they have. He is able to give to others because he does not consume so much for himself.

10 In the *Acts of Paul and Thecla,* which was written over a century after this time, Paul is described as 'a short man but of good bodily state, semi-bald but with eyebrows meeting and a semi-hooked nose, and crooked in the legs yet full of grace. Sometimes he appeared like a man and sometimes he had the face of an angel.' As this was written long after his death we cannot be sure of its accuracy; however, as it does not paint a picture of a man with attractive physical features there may be something behind it.

In chapter 11 Paul lists some of the suffering he endured for Christ. Travel was always dangerous but once Roman rule was established in the area travelling conditions improved. Rome had reduced the risk of encountering pirates and had built straight roads which made it much more difficult for bandits to operate. However, it is obvious from Paul's experience that safety could not be assured.

12:7 There has been much speculation about the 'thorn in the flesh'. We do not know, but it could have been malaria which was common in the low-lying coastal areas. It is like a red hot bar thrust through the forehead and leaves one weak for many days. This would certainly have inhibited Paul's work.

Site History and Visits

Kavala

History

Kavala was founded in about the sixth century BC by people from Thassos who called it Neapolis – a name it still retained in the time of Paul. Before the rise of Macedonia it was allied to Athens. It was granted city status by the Romans in 168 BC. Brutus and Cassius used it as a base for their fleet in the Battle of Philippi 42 BC. It continued to grow in importance because of its place at the end of the Via Egnatia.

In Byzantine times it was a major Christian base and renamed Christoupolis. Justinian (sixth century AD) began extensive fortifications against the raids from the north. It was captured and sacked in 1185 by the Crusaders.

From 1387 to 1912 it was part of the Ottoman Empire. The Byzantine fortress on the Panagian hill was extended. The old Roman aquaduct was rebuilt and extended by Suleiman the Magnificant and still dominates the view of the town from the bay.

In 1919 many Greeks from western Turkey moved to Kavala following the relocations at the end of the First World War and the town prospered. It was temporally in Bulgarian control during the Second World War from 1941– 44.

Visit

Kavala today is a fine mixture of old and new. The setting of the moon shaped bay with the buildings behind gives the impression of a large amphitheatre. On the west side of Kavala there are modern buildings and shops but the Panagia area on the eastern side is still one of narrow streets and old buildings. Many of these houses are very well maintained. The Imaret, an old building with eighteen domes, is now a café. The archaeological museum contains a good collection of finds from Amphipolis as well as those from Philippi and Kavala.

St Thomas' Church is situated in the old quarter near the harbour. Outside, on the harbour side is a recent statue commemorating the place where Paul and his companions could have landed and set foot in Europe. The old harbour too has many colourful fishermen's boats and it is well worth spending time walking along the quayside.

Philippi

History

Philippi is located ten miles from Neapolis, separated from the coast by the Symbolon mountains. To the east is Mt Orbelos and to the west Mt Pangaeum. It is on a flat plain which in the past has been marshy but reclamation today makes it a good area for agriculture.

Gold was discovered at Mount Pangaeus and the early inhabitants from the island of Thrace were attracted to it for this reason. They called the settlement, which they founded in about 360 BC, Krenides from *krenai* – a spring. In spite of some of the ground being waterlogged, the site had a key asset – water.

Soon afterwards the inhabitants sought help from Philip of Macedon against the Thraceans. He assisted them and renamed the settlement Philippi. He fortified the growing town and traces of his walls can still be found on the acropolis. Philip made the town a 'free city' but received a yearly tax of 1,000 talents of gold. This income enabled him to extend his rule in the area. An early theatre was constructed and may have been in use in Paul's day. The present theatre dates back to the time of Marcus Aurelius (second century AD) and may have held up to 50,000 people.

Philippi was sited on the Via Egnatia, which was completed in 130 BC. It meant that it was a useful staging post for soldiers travelling to or from the east. The major battle which was the death knell for the Roman Republic took place near Philippi, Cassius and Brutus being defeated by Octavian (Augustus) and Mark Anthony. After the battle the Republican troops were dispossessed of their Italian property (Dio Cassius 50:4) and were settled in Philippi. Later, when Anthony was defeated by Octavian and Agrippa at nearby Actium in 31 BC, some of Anthony's troops from Italy were also settled in Philippi. So the city, now renamed Colonia Julia Augusta Philippensis, continued to grow and maintain strong links with Italy. The colony had *ius italicum* status, which meant it had the same rights as Italian cities and was exempt from direct taxation. The official language was Latin and this is seen on most of the inscriptions that have been found there. However, Greek was widely understood and used.

Extensive repairs to the Via Egnatia took place in the reigns of Trajan and Hadrian between AD 97 and 138. The forum, which dates from the time of Marcus Aurelius (AD 161-180), runs parallel to and south of the Via Egnatia. It is about 150 metres by 70 metres, and is almost certainly built on the site of the forum Paul knew. To the west of the city on the Via Egnatia is a commemorative arch celebrating the boundary of the city, and then after a further mile the road crossed the River Gangites.

A half century after Paul, Ignatius of Antioch passed through Philippi on his way to martyrdom in Rome. The Philippians asked Bishop Polycarp of Smyrna for help in collecting Ignatius' letters and an encouraging response from Polycarp agrees to their request.

Philippi continued to be the see of a bishop. The Slavs invaded in the seventh century and the Bulgarians in 812, whilst it came under Ottoman rule in 1387.

Philippi was first excavated by the French in 1856, then again in 1914 and 1920-37. Since then the University of Thessalonica has continued the task. Five churches have been excavated within the ruins, including one that might date from the fourth century near the river site associated with the place of prayer.

Visit

Guides vary in the order of the visit, so I have kept to the order in which the sites are mentioned in the Bible.

The River Gangites is closer to the site in the north, and here a venue has been developed beside a small church and some trees where pilgrims can remember, maybe even by renewing their own baptismal vows, the baptism by Paul of the first recorded converts in Europe.

Between the river and the site of Philippi is a commemorative arch marking the western boundary of the former city.

Near the entrance to the forum can be seen some remains of the Via Egnatia. Then in the middle of the forum on the north side are four steps which would have led to the judgment seat (bema) at which Paul was judged. The forum was surrounded by colonnades and some of these pillars still stand. To the west was the temple dedicated to the worship of Emperor Antoninus Pius. The main shopping area, commercial agora, was to the south (there being insufficient room between the Via Egnatia and the forum for them in the north). There also is the palestra and the remains of a sixth-century church. Four brick pillars still stand, and some pillars erected in the tenth century formed the narthex. Also in this area are the fairly well preserved remains of the public latrines.

At the east end of the forum was the library, but the visible remains are those of a fifth-century church in an octagonal shape. This may have been built on the site of an earlier church as there is a mosaic dedicated to St Paul by the fourth-century bishop Porphirios. In this area there are some houses, including one for the bishop, and public baths.

To the north of the modern road are the remains of a fifth-century church and at the west end of this is a crypt which was thought to be Paul's prison because, at its discovery in 1876, there could be seen murals of Paul in prison.

PHILIPPI

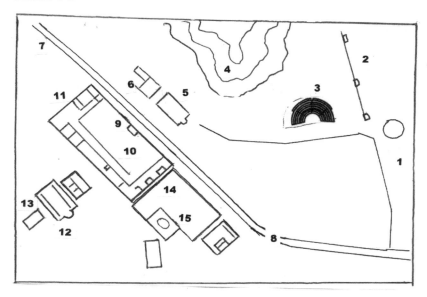

1.	Parking	6.	'Pauls Prison'	11.	Temple
2.	City walls	7.	To Lydia Baptism site	12.	Church
3.	Theatre	8.	Via Egnatia	13.	Latrines
4.	Acropolis	9.	Bema	14.	Library
5.	Basilica	10.	Forum	15.	Octagonal church

Thessalonica

History

The town was first called Therma after the hot springs in the area. That name was retained as a district of Thessalonica when it was founded by Cassander in 315 BC. Cassander had married Thessa Jonica, the daughter of Philip of Macedon and sister of Alexander the Great, and was one of Alexander's generals.

Thessalonica was in a very good location, built on the slope of Mt Khortiatis on the western side of the Chalcidic peninsula in the Thermaic Gulf. As at Neapolis the hillside forms a natural amphitheatre. On the top of Mt Khortiatis was the citadel. All around Thessalonica is a fertile alluvial plain built up by deposits from the Vardar and Vistritza rivers. It rapidly became and continues to be the main seaport of Macedonia. Livy mentions it as the base for the Macedonian navy during the war between Rome and Persia. In 146 BC the Romans made Thessalonica the capital of the new Province of Macedonia.

It became a free city in 42 BC for supporting Anthony and Octavia in the Battle of Philippi. In New Testament times it was by far the largest and most important city of Macedonia. It was a key harbour and city on the Egnatian way.

Little remains of the city Paul knew. There are parts of the Roman city wall which would date back to his time. The arch of Galerius, erected at the beginning of the fourth century as the eastern gate on the Egnatian way, shows some of his victories over the Persians. The western or Vardar gate was demolished in 1876 so that its stone could be used to repair the city wall. However, there is an inscription from it in the British Museum which contains the word 'politarch', the name Luke gives to the officials in Paul's day. The title seems to have been in use from about 30 BC to AD 140 and first-century inscriptions have been found showing its use in places like Beroea. It is not used anywhere else and shows how accurate Luke was in his historical detail. Of interest, although unlikely to be the same person, is that among those listed on the gate inscription as politarchs is Secundus (Acts 20:4) .

Thessalonica became the capital of the first of two divisions into which Macedonia was divided by Diocletian (AD 284–305). Emperor Galerius established his palace in Thessalonica in 305. In 390 Emperor Theodosius ordered the massacre of seven thousand citizens for insurrection. For several centuries the city successfully warded off the attacks of various enemies, and for this it was known as 'the Orthodox city' because it was a bulwark guarding Christianity and Byzantine civilization against the attacks of the barbarians from the north. Indeed it seems to have played an important part in the conversions among these tribes.

In 904 it was captured by the Saracens, who killed or took as prisoners a large number of the inhabitants and burned much of the city. Another massacre occurred when the city was taken by the Norman Crusaders in 1185. Subsequently in 1204 Boniface of Monferrat made it his capital. In 1430 Sultan Amurath II captured it, and it remained under Turkish rule until the Greeks captured it in 1912. It became a base for the Allies in World War I but much of it was destroyed by a fire in 1917, including the Church of St Demetrios. The Germans captured and held it for three and a half years during the Second World War.

Visit

The city walls date from the earliest days but most of what is seen today dates from the time of Sinan in the first half of the sixteenth century. They include the Arch of Galerius, erected in AD 304 to commemorate his victory over the Persians in 297. Perhaps the most famous part of the city fortifications is the White Tower by the harbour. It was built in the 15th century. During Ottoman occupation it became the place for executions. When the Greeks captured Thessalonika they whitewashed it to blot out the blood stains and gave it this new name. It now houses the Museum of History and Art.

Near the Arch of Galerius is the Church of St George, which began life in the fourth century as a Pantheum or Mausoleum for Galerius, hence its rotunda shape. It then became a Christian church. The Turks used it as a mosque and its minaret is still there. The Greeks rededicated it to St George. It contains some fine mosaics especially those depicting birds: ducks, partridges and peacocks. There are also life-like depictions of soldier-saints.

St Dimitrios Church, with its five aisles, was destroyed in the great fire of 1917 and rebuilt in 1948. It is built on the site where the Roman baths once stood and is Greece's largest church. Agios Dimitrios is the patron saint of Thessaloniki and this church houses some spectacular mosaics. The crypt on the east end of the church is the place in the Roman baths where Saint Dimitrios was tortured and killed by Roman soldiers.

Just to the south of this church is Law Court Square, where in 1962 the central bus station was removed and work began on excavating the area known as Dikastiria. A second-century forum was found, most likely built above the area where Jason and some early Christians may have been dragged before the local magistrates. Below the pavement of the partly preserved small theatre was found a first-century bathhouse and a mint. In the south-west corner is the small church of Panayia Halkeon. It contains a few icons and in the Ottoman era it was used as a mosque for coppersmiths.

Panayia Ahiropitos is the oldest church in Thessalonica. It dates from the fifth century and has some finely carved columns and some mosaics of birds and fruit.

The church of St Sofia dates from the eighth century. It was built on the model of the Church of San Sofia in Constantinople. Below the church is a Roman *nymphaeum* that was re-dedicated in the Christian era as the Well of John the Baptist. The magnificent Pantocrator icon in the ten metre dome of St Sofia has round it the words from Acts 1:11, 'Men of Galilee why to you stand here looking into the sky?' Typically, icons of the virgin with angels and the apostles circle the icon of ascended Christ.

The Archaeological Museum is well worth a visit. Its most important display is a vast collection of gold, silver and bronze from the Macedonian era. Among them are crowns and other jewellery, bowls, and artifacts.

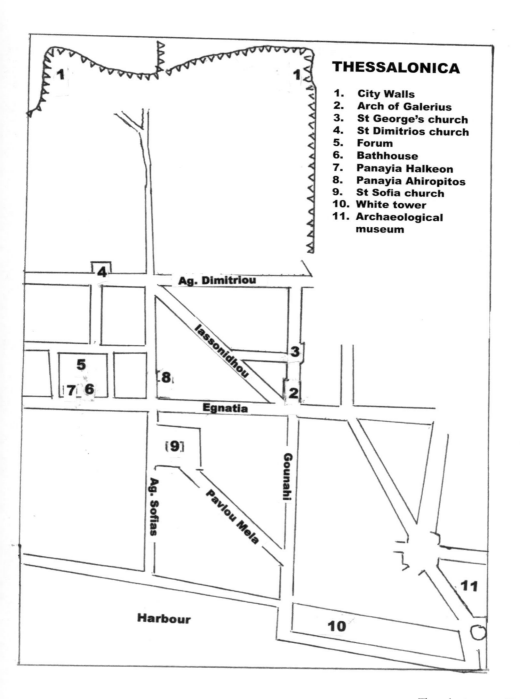

THESSALONICA

1. City Walls
2. Arch of Galerius
3. St George's church
4. St Dimitrios church
5. Forum
6. Bathhouse
7. Panayia Halkeon
8. Panayia Ahiropitos
9. St Sofia church
10. White tower
11. Archaeological museum

Veria (Berea)

After Paul's time Berea remained a fairly large city. Its bishop was at first under the Metropolitan of Thessalonica but later, in the time of Andronicus II (1283–1328), it had its own metropolitan.

The town defended itself against the Bulgarians and Serbs but was conquered by the Ottoman Turks in 1373. Under Ottoman rule, up to fifty churches were built but were 'hidden' from view so that a casual visitor walking down a street would not realize there was a church behind what looked like a garden wall. It appears that during Turkish rule the authorities knew of these churches and the town's reputation for being a 'little Jerusalem'. As long as the churches remained hidden and with high windows which made them look like warehouses or barns, the authorities were willing to turn a blind eye.

In the last thirty years many of the interesting features of the town have been removed, so it is no longer a place for discovering what is hidden behind the garden wall.

Some of these churches can still be entered, although only one is regularly open to visitors.

Near the twelfth-century cathedral is an ancient tree where in 1430 the Ottomans hanged Archbishop Arsenios.

The Church of Anastasseos Christou celebrates the Resurrection of Christ. Some of its frescoes have been restored. Among these are the Dormition and Assumption over the west door; on the north wall is an interesting interpretation of the Crucifixion with Jesus using a ladder to climb onto the cross ; and on the south wall is a picture of the Transfiguration with one of the disciples falling over backwards in astonishment.

Other churches well worth a visit, if time and the keys can be found, are St Christos, St Kyrikos, and St Stephanos.

There is a Byzantine Museum with a very good collection of icons in a restored nineteenth-century flour mill. Flour milling along with tanning were major industries in Veria.

Athens

History

Athens is five miles inland from the port of Piraeus. It is on a narrow plain between Mount Hymettus in the south, Mount Pentelicus in the east and Mount Parnes in the north. Legend claims it was founded by Theseus, who slew the Minotaur and conquered the Amazons. It was named in honour of the goddess Athena.

At around 600 BC Solon tried to bring in reforms which encouraged commercial enterprise and agriculture but his attempts towards democracy failed, although there seems to have been a move towards the equalization of the classes. There followed a half century of despotic rule under Peisistratus and his sons. It was a time of prosperity during which Athens began to become a dominant power in the region.

In 508 BC Cleisthenes, who had taken a leading part in driving out the 'tyrants', produced a constitution which makes him the true founder of Athenian democracy. He gave the franchise to all Athenians and set up the popular assembly (*ecclesia*) and the council (*boule*).

In the fifth century BC Athens played a major role in resisting the Persian invasion under Themistocles and Miltiades. Wealthy citizens were commandeered to fund the cost of the ships, its fleet being a major contribution towards the defeat of the Persians.

Athens reached its peak of influence in the time of Pericles (died 429 BC). The Delian Confederacy was under Athenian leadership. It had a fleet of around 300 ships and an army of 30,000 trained soldiers. In the last fifteen years of Pericles, the Parthenon and other major buildings were constructed. This too was the time when Athens was a major influence in philosophy, science, and literature. Scholars from all over the world came to see this democratic state.

No sooner had Athens reached its zenith than other jealous states in the Delian Confederacy joined up with Sparta to bring about its destruction. The Peloponnesian war (431– 404 BC) ruined Athens. Although stripped of its political and military influence, Athens kept its philosophical dominance, which was never again equalled in ancient times.

Philip of Macedonia conquered Athens in 338 BC, but he and his son Alexander admired their culture and encouraged the Athenians to work with them in the defeat of the Persians. There followed a hundred years in which Macedonian rule varied in its dominance. By now the seeds of Athens decline were evident. Alexandria was becoming the centre for science and scholarship and Athens was falling into its state of barren philosophical discussion.

Athens had had friendly relations with Rome since 228 BC, so when the Romans conquered in 146 BC they left the declining city free to continue being a centre of philosophy. Sadly some of its leaders felt snubbed by their loss of importance, and the philosopher Ariston's attempt at outright rebellion led to the city being taken by Sulla in 86 BC. The soldiers looted the city but did not damage the main buildings. The city was now poverty-stricken but retained its schools of philosophy which were even attended by trendy young Romans like Cicero and Horace.

In the Roman civil war at the beginning of the empire, Athens always sided with the wrong side and Augustus stripped it of any remaining powers that it claimed.

In the time of the early church Athens showed its gratitude for being allowed to continue as a 'free city' by enthusiastic emperor worship. Nero was fond of the place and under the Antonines it was given the status of a university. After Constantine, Athens retained its role as a centre of learning and some of the early church fathers, such as Basil and Gregory of Nazianzus, were among its alumni. In 529 Justinian forbade the study of philosophy and Athens is hardly mentioned in the centuries that follow until it was ruled by the Crusaders between 1204 and 1458.

In 1458 it came under Ottoman rule. Some attempts were made to liberate it by the Venetians and the most notable result of this was the ruin of the Parthenon by the explosions of gunpowder being stored by the Ottomans. In 1645 the explosion was caused by a lightning strike and in 1687 the gunpowder was ignited by a Venetian shell. The Venetians and then the Turks used much of the temple stone for repairing the city walls, especially in 1778. In 1833 it was made the capital of the new Kingdom of Greece.

Greece declared war on Turkey in 1912 and consolidated lands already won over from Turkish rule. Athens was taken by the Germans during the Second World War. Since that time the city has once more flourished as the capital of Greece, so it is hard to imagine that for 2,000 years until 200 years ago it was like a small market town.

Visit

Agora

Many now believe that Paul visited and witnessed in the agora and it is not so likely that he was brought before a counsel on Mars Hill. The western market by Paul's time was virtually a museum of temples and statues. Petronius remarked that 'it was easier to find a god than a man in Athens'. That fits in well with Paul's comment about the 'unknown god'.

The Temple of Hephaistos, the patron of metalworkers and blacksmiths, is a good site to get an overall picture of the agora. It was converted in the Byzantine era to the church of St George. The church of the Holy Apostles contains some interesting frescos.

The eastern sector of the agora was the place for commercial activity. It was just over 100 metres square and the centre of city life. In this area is the Tower of the Winds, a huge water clock, sundial and weathervane consisting of an octagonal marble tower with marble sculptures of the eight winds at its top.

In the 1950s the Americans reconstructed the Stoa of Attalos which contains a museum.

The Acropolis

The Christians changed the Parthenon into a church dedicated to San Sophia and there are still some faint remains of icons on the west wall. During the Crusades it became a catholic church dedicated to Notre Dame. The Ottomans turned it into a mosque but the building was ruined in 1687. The Ottomans were using it as a gunpowder store and during the Venetian invasion a cannonball fell on the building, causing a massive explosion. The illustration below shows how it is thought the Acropolis looked before the Venetian siege.

The present Parthenon, a temple for Athena, the protector of Athens, was built in the time of Pericles on a site that had contained a temple from the sixth century BC. A second building was erected around 490 BC soon after the battle of Marathon but was destroyed by the Persians.

The Periclean Parthenon is the work of the architect Ictinos and was erected in around 440 BC. It is a simple building surrounded by one row of Doric columns. Ictinos used various methods, like changing the thickness of the columns and the curve of the steps, to give such an inspiring look to the building.

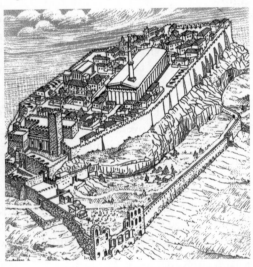

Athens in the seventeenth century

The removal of some of the sculptured metropes (rectangular slabs above the architrave) by Lord Byron certainly preserved them but is still a cause of contention. One of those remaining is on the north-west corner and shows a Centaur (half-horse, half-man) seizing a Lapith by the neck and ready to administer a fatal blow.

At the east end of the Parthenon was the Temple of Rome and Augustus, built soon after 27 BC. Thirteen small altars to Augustus have been found in the lower city.

The other main feature of the Acropolis is the Erechtheion. The name comes from the Attic king Erechtheus, who was later merged into the sea-god Poseidon. The design is very complicated because it had to incorporate various older sanctuaries. Much of the layout was changed when it became a Christian church in the seventh century. Although the eye is naturally on the portico of the Caryatids – pillars carved in the shape of females guarding the tomb of Erechtheion – it is important not to miss the fine decorations like that on the south wall.

THE ACROPOLIS

1. **Propylaea**
2. **Sanctuary of Artemis**
3. **Parthenon**
4. **Temple of Rome**
5. **Altar of Athens**
6. **Erechtheum**

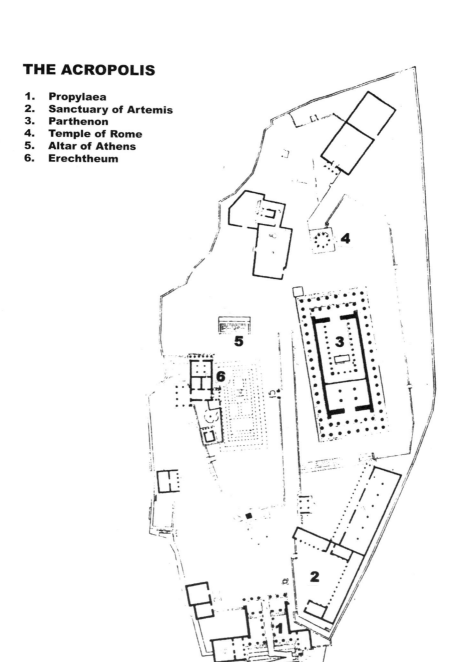

Corinth

History

Corinth (named after a type of grape) may have begun as a Phoenician settlement, although some signs of habitation have been found as far back as the fourth millennium BC. In the time of Homer it was under the Myceneans. At this time worship of the sea-god Poseidon took precedence. Corinth's sea power extended during the eighth to seventh centuries BC with colonies at Corcyra and Syracuse. Its prosperity grew from that time and in the sixth century it took over as the main trader between east and west, holding trading agreements with Egypt, Cyprus and what is now Turkey.

Corinth was well known for its bronze and pottery which was exported throughout the Mediterranean. The desire for commercial wealth led to the neglect of its military, but for mutual defence it joined the Peloponnesian League under Sparta while retaining much of its independence.

In the Persian war of 480 BC, Corinth served as the Greek headquarters; its army took part at the battle of Thermopylae and its navy at Salamis and Mycale. When its position of trade was threatened by Athens, Corinth attacked by land and sea but was defeated. In 432 BC Corinth joined forces with Sparta to attack Athens. There followed many years of changing alliances and struggle until Philip of Macedon took control and left a garrison on the citadel. Later there were attempts to break free from Macedonian rule and opposition to Roman influence.

After its conquest of 146 BC, Roman forces under Lucius Mummius sacked Corinth, killed its male population, sold its women and children into slavery and took away its treasures. In 46 BC Julius Caesar, realizing its strategic importance, resettled Corinth as a Roman colony with Italian freedmen and dispossessed Greeks. From then on it rapidly recovered its prosperity and Augustus made it the capital of Achaea.

Corinth was dominated by the Acropolis. At 575 metres (1890ft) it was able to control the isthmus to the Peloponnese, which is only five miles across. Anyone travelling north to south passed through the city. The sea route round Cape

Malea was very dangerous (the Cape Horn of the day) so for many centuries goods and sometimes small ships were taken across the isthmus.

In the time of Paul it was the major city of the province and a thriving sea port. Athenaeus, who lived a century before Paul's visit, said it had a population of around 200,000 citizens and double that number of slaves. The circumference of the walled city was six miles.

Although Greek was the common language, Latin was used on inscriptions, with only about 3 per cent of inscriptions from the time being in Greek. Eight of the seventeen names of Christians in Corinth are Latin: Aquila, Priscilla, Titus Justus, Fortunatus, Gaius, Lucius, Quartus, Tertius. Greek names are Chloe, Stephanas, Sosipater, Sosthenes, Achaicus, Erastus, Jason, Crispus, and Phoebe.

Visit

Paul, arriving from Athens, would have noticed the major difference. Athens was a city living on the past and its buildings showed considerable signs of wear. From 46 BC Corinth had been rebuilt as a Roman colony. Some of the major buildings were still under construction. The whole city had a feeling of newness about it.

Most visitors reached the city by the road from Lechaeum, which was built from limestone blocks with a raised walkway on each side. As this road approached the agora it was flanked on both sides by small shops which opened either on to the street or on to a courtyard.

Reconstruction of the north side of the agora by H D Wood

A basilica, a large columned hall used by the Romans for commercial and judicial purposes, stood on the west side just before the road entered the agora. The Peribolos of Apollo was opposite it on the east side of the road. This was a large paved court surrounded by columns and containing a large statue of Apollo.

Corinth's most important reservoir, the Fountain of Peirene, was constructed between the Peribolos of Apollo and the agora. This reservoir had a capacity of over 81,000 gallons (306,500 litres) and was fed by subterranean waters led in by many tunnels from the east and west.

In this area were the baths and the fish market. A large water tank was used to store live fish until they were selected for sale.

The road from Lechaeum entered the agora from the north through the propylaea, or entrance, a staircase surmounted by a magnificent gateway. Though it comes from a later century, the discovery by archaeologists in this area of a piece of white marble with the inscription 'Synagogue of the Hebrews' suggests that the synagogue may have been located somewhere in the vicinity. The main shops were on the north and west sides of the agora, and a doorstep inscribed 'Lucius the Butcher' was found in a shop in the agora.

A 150-metre stoa, or colonnaded pavilion, was in the south. To the rear of this were many small shops equipped with pits cooled by water brought from the Fountain of Peirene through underground channels. These may have been restaurants or wine shops using the cool waters as a means of refrigeration. Leading out from the middle of this stoa was the road to Cenchreae, the harbour where Paul departed from Corinth.

The *bouleuterion*, meeting place of the council, was on the west side of this road and another basilica was on the east. On the eastern edge of the agora was a large building which has been called the 'Julian Basilica' but whose use is unknown. The large open plaza of the agora was divided by a row of shops running east and west. In the centre of these was the bema, an ornate structure covered with sculptured marble, where public officials would address the populace. There were benches for the dignitaries and rooms for those waiting to present their cases to the magistrate. This is likely to be the place where Paul was brought before the governor Gallio (Acts 18:12-17).

Another road led from the agora north-west to Sicyon. To the east of this road and just north of the agora was the site of what was thought to be the temple of

Apollo. There is now considerable evidence to suggest that this was the temple of Athena. It was one of the oldest in Greece and in Paul's time it had recently been restored. Seven massive Doric columns from this structure, which are still standing, are the most striking remains of ancient Corinth. Alongside a temple on the west of this road was the Fountain of Glauke, an important princess in Corinthian mythology.

At the west end of the forum there was a huge temple built for emperor worship in the time of Tiberius (AD 14-37). It is further evidence of the shift away from the old gods to Emperor worship at that time.

The temple of Asclepius (the god of healing) was built just inside the northern city wall on the west side of the road. A number of buildings for the patients surrounded this temple and an elaborate system of water storage and supply indicates the importance of water in effecting the cures. In it have been found reproductions of the parts of the body for which healing was sought. They include legs and feet, arms and hands and sexual organs.

The Odeion, or music hall, and a large theatre were located in the north-western sector of the city. A reused paving block found near the theatre bears the name of an Erastus who was Commissioner of Public Works. It has been suggested that this was none other than the associate of Paul mentioned in Acts 19:22 and Romans 16:23. Temples have also been found to Isis and Serapis, Demeter, Artemis, Helius, Pelagrina, Hera, Dionysius, Poseidon, Necessity, Fates, Maid, Zeus, and Hermes.

According to Strabo, the temple of Aphrodite on the Acropolis 'owned a thousand temple-slaves, prostitutes, who had been dedicated to the goddess'. However, Strabo points out that the temple was small. Excavations have revealed foundations roughly 10 metres by 16 metres. Coins of the day depict this temple.

Corinth's location near the scene of the Isthmian Games is significant in the light of Paul's frequent reference to athletics in his Corinthian letters. A gymnasium consisted of the *dromos* – a track for running – and the *palaistra* – an open court for wrestling. A variety of rooms led off the *palaistra*, like the oil-anointing room, washrooms, and sometimes lecture theatres. Under Roman rule the gymnasia moved towards being educational establishments where there were libraries and the various sports were taught, rather than places of competition.

CORINTH

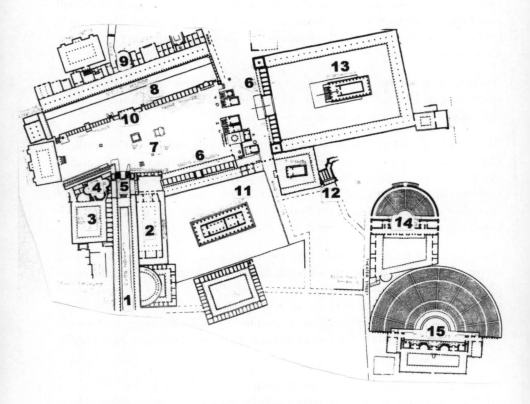

1. Lechaion Road
2. Basilica
3. Peribolos of Apollo
4. Fountain of Peirene
5. Propylaea
6. Shops
7. Agora
8. Stoa
9. Bouleuterion
10. Bema
11. Temple of Athena
12. Fountain of Glauke
13. Temple to the
    emperor
14. Odeion
15. Theatre

The Orthodox Church

The Church Year and Daily Faith

The Church year It is claimed that an Orthodox Christian lives each day very much in the presence of Christ. Easter is the hinge on which the whole Orthodox year hangs. It is the key feast in the church and the year becomes one of a journey from Easter to Easter.

The church year begins in September and besides the key time of Holy Week and Easter there are twelve other festivals:

The Birth of Mary	September 8
The Exaltation of the Cross	September 14
Jesus in the Temple	November 21
Christmas	About two weeks after Dec.25
The Epiphany	" " " our date
The Meeting	February 2
The Annunciation	March 25

Palm Sunday	
EASTER	
The Ascension	
Pentecost	
Transfiguration	August 6
The Dormition of Mary	August 15

The day that follows each of these special feasts is linked (synaxis) with another appropriate day. So the day after the Birth of Mary is dedicated to Joachim and Anna, her parents. The day after Jesus in the Temple is dedicated to those who blessed him there – Simeon and Anna. The day after the Annunciation is dedicated to the Archangel Gabriel, who came to Mary.

Because of its overriding importance, Easter is anticipated by ten weeks of preparation and forty days of celebration afterwards until the Ascension. Other feasts have one or more days, before or after, linked to the festival.

The encounter The word 'today' often comes in the liturgy and hymns of these great festivals. The idea is that we actually relive in the present the great events. The past joins the present. Through them a real encounter takes place between us and Christ. He is born in my soul, he hangs on the cross for me, I share in his resurrection, he ascends and I ascend with him. Christ is the eternally present one – the same yesterday, today and for ever (Hebrews 13:8).

> The Orthodox Church's liturgical year is ... A sermon on the mystery of divine love, and this sermon is preached in words more powerful and sublime than any that could come from the preacher. (F.Heiler, Urkirche ... Ostkirche.)

'Next to the miraculous and gracious providence of God, I ascribe the preservation of Christianity to the strict and devout observance of the Festivals.' (T. Smith in 'An Account of the Greek Church', commenting on the strength of faith among the Orthodox after centuries of persecution from Islam.)

Daily faith

Each day of the week is set aside for a specific theme.

Sunday is a little Easter, the day to remember the resurrection of Jesus. A positive note is struck at the beginning of each week which will carry us through the days ahead. We begin each week by celebrating the greatest victory ever won in this world.

Monday is set aside to remember God's protection for us and his unseen rule through archangels, angels and hosts of invisible powers.

Tuesday is dedicated to John the Baptist, the last of the Old Testament prophets who prepared the way for Christ.

Wednesday is considered to be the day when Judas decided to betray Jesus. It is a day of fasting.

Thursday is a day to remember the Apostles and Church Fathers.

Friday is a fast day when we remember Christ's death on the cross.

Saturday is dedicated to the martyrs and other Christians who are with Christ in glory. It is the day Jesus raised Lazarus from the dead and the day Jesus rested in the tomb from his work. So it is an appropriate day to remember the dead in Christ.

Just as the week is divided, so is the day.

Each day in Orthodox devotion starts at 6am and still follows the day as it was in the Bible and still is in many lands.

7 am: the first hour after sunrise has the theme of the coming of light and so reminds us of the coming of the Light of the World. Physical light is but an icon of the light of Christ. So we praise God for the glory of light seen in the face of Christ. We pray that that light will guide us through the day ahead.

9 am is remembered as the time when the Holy Spirit came upon the disciples on the day of Pentecost. In churches and monasteries three psalms are read, including Psalm 51 which in verses 10-11 expresses our need for the Holy Spirit:

Create in me a pure heart, O God, and renew a steadfast
spirit within me.
Do not cast me from your presence or take your Holy
Spirit from me.

It reminds us that without the Holy Spirit our life is empty of inner peace and power, for he is the one in whom we live and have our being (Acts 17:28).

The sixth hour or noon is the time when Jesus was crucified for us. So we offer up prayers for thanksgiving for all that Jesus did for us and pray that he will save us from the sins that so easily take over our life.

The ninth hour (3pm) is the time when Jesus died. We rejoice that by his death he destroyed death and pray that we might put to death our old sinful nature and live our new life (Colossians 3).

Sunset is the time to remind ourselves that Jesus came to be a light in our dark world. The darkness of sin and death makes us long for the light. The early Greek hymn Φως ιλαρον (O gladsome light), from the second century, picks up this theme.

Midnight is to remember that at this hour the Jews were liberated by the angel from Egypt. Jesus talked of returning at such an hour and from the early church it has been associated with the Second Coming. In some monasteries the monks rise at midnight, as if from the bed of death, to meet the Lord in prayer. Orthodox members are encouraged to use any time they wake in the night to meet, in prayer, their risen ascended Lord. A far better activity than worrying about the next day!

Prayer

According to the Eastern Church, doctrine is shaped by prayer and prayer by doctrine. The great Fathers of the church formulated their faith from their experience of God in prayer and in the Bible. The doctrine of the Church is not only expressed through prayer; it comes from prayer. Prayer is the uniting of heart, mind and body with God. The sacraments are the way to *theosis*, becoming like God, since they make us partakers of divine nature. There is no limit to the number of sacraments, for a sacrament happens whenever God's grace is mediated to man through matter. 'Traditionally the Orthodox understand everything in the church to be sacramental. All of life becomes a sacrament in Christ who fills life itself with the Spirit of God' (Father Thomas Hopko). All the sacraments and all the theology of the church flow from prayer. Life is a sacrament because God has taken a body and this fundamental doctrine of the Incarnation is revealed in life and prayer. Because Christ is God himself, nothing is higher than him. The Incarnation is, therefore, very important. Deification is what God wants for mankind; God offers us his very life through Christ and the Holy Spirit; I in them, they in me.

Life and prayer, then, are sacramental. At the end of the day, when one prays, those prayers will tell you how you have spent your day. If the day has been spent watching horror-movies, then your prayer will be affected. It is vital to ask God to be with you at the beginning of each day so that his will can be done. In fact, throughout the whole day one is to be conscious of prayer. To be aware of God's presence and to be vigilant so that you do not let in negative thoughts or sinful deeds is very important. If negative thoughts occur, then you put your mind on God or concentrate on what you are doing, like stirring the soup, so that you have purity of thought throughout the day, making the heart ready for the indwelling of grace by constantly guarding its inner purity. How, then, is this inner purity to be attained? It is through the abiding of the Most Holy Trinity in the soul in accordance with the words of Jesus, 'We will come to him and make our home in him.' Only life according to the commandments leads to God, combined with a life in the Spirit of God.

Union with God cannot take place outside of prayer, for prayer is a personal relationship with God. The personal aspect of God is fundamental and because of this the prayer life of a child can be deeper than that of a lazy Patriarch.

In prayer, then, one meets with God personally; it is to know and to love him; knowledge (gnosis) and love are closely interconnected in Eastern asceticism. Prayer is 'to stand with the mind in the heart before God, and to go on standing before Him unceasingly day and night, until the end of life' (Theophan the Recluse). If we remain with the mind in the head, we will be relying on the human intellect and we will never have an immediate and personal encounter with God. In prayer, then, there must be a descent from the head into the heart. The head seeks God, but it is the heart that finds him. The heart is the Lord's reception room. 'The kingdom of God is within you', said Jesus.

The importance of prayer is to be seen in the life of Jesus, where almost every great event was preceded by prayer: e.g. the Baptism, the Transfiguration, the call of the disciples. The two great movements in the life of Jesus were the withdrawal into God's presence for prayer and the return into the world strengthened to do God's will. Furthermore, it is because of the Incarnation that Matter is very important. There is no separation of material and spiritual reality. So cars, houses and wedding rings are all blessed. When water is blessed it is not only symbolic but also the water itself is bearing the grace physically. Monastic clothes are blessed on the altar, and when these or any other matter is blessed, like the food at meal times, it is the actual matter that is blessed, not just asking for some grace. These prayers are not seen as idolizing matter: they are to do with the Creator God who has made all things and the Incarnate God who regards the body as being important and takes bodily sins seriously. At memorial services, sweetmeats and wheat are blessed to signify the dying to self and the bringing forth of fruit. In Christ, God knows and has entered into hunger and thirst and his most intimate communication is through eating – his Body and Blood. Our body is the temple of the Spirit of God so it has to be treated with reverence. If you hit wood, you get a wooden sound; if you hit glass, it is a glass sound; whatever hits a Christian should make them resound with the sound of the gospel!

The Jesus Prayer

This is one of the most famous prayers of the Orthodox Church and is prayed by all. It is easy to remember and continually repeated at each drawing of breath so as to become second nature: 'Lord Jesus Christ, have mercy on me, a sinner.' It calls on the name of Jesus and acknowledges him as the Son of God; it addresses us as sinners so as to cover every situation. It is a profession of faith which is a summing up of the Gospels. It is Trinitarian in that Jesus is the Son of the Father and no one can recognize in the prophet of Galilee the Incarnate Son of God unless the Holy Spirit teaches him to see, to understand and to commit himself. The repetition does not make the interior life mechanical and mindless: on the contrary, it frees it and turns it towards contemplation by constantly driving away, from the region of the heart, the effect of sin and every external thought or image. The object of spiritual prayer is the fire of grace which enters the heart; the Jesus prayer gives the possibility that this may be received, by recollecting the thoughts and making ready the soul before the Lord. The essential thing is to hold oneself ready before God, calling out to him from the depths of one's heart.

If you see God you do not need any icons; therefore, icons are not an obligation in prayer. But if one is not seeing God directly then it is difficult to be sure that any images we have are leading us to God. Icons are used in prayer as a way to link the worshipper with God. We can only be sure to see the face of God Incarnate, in Christ. Material images can be made of him who took a material body. But now that God has appeared in the flesh and lived among men, I make an image of the God who can be seen. I do not worship matter, but I worship the Creator of matter, who for my sake became material and deigned to dwell in matter, who through matter effected my salvation. I will not cease from worshipping the matter through which my salvation has been effected. God has 'deified' matter, making it 'spirit-bearing', and if flesh becomes a vehicle of the Spirit, then so, in a different way, can wood and paint. The Orthodox doctrine of icons is bound up with the Orthodox belief that the whole of God's creation, material as well as spiritual, is to be redeemed and glorified. 'The artistic perfection of an icon was not only a reflection of the celestial glory – it was a concrete example of matter restored to its original harmony and beauty, and serving as a vehicle of the Spirit' (Nicholas Zernov, 1898-1980). One can pray, then, either with one's eyes shut concentrating on the heart, the centre of one's being, or concentrating on an icon of Christ because he has a painted, visible face that is real: 'He who has seen me has seen the Father'. God is seen as a man in Christ and the icon is a way of relating to this real person. The icon shows the Body transfigured by the Spirit and communicates the Spirit to the one who looks. Using an icon in prayer brings you into the Presence of the person. To kiss the icon of Christ is to know that God is accepting veneration as surely as if you were kissing his hand. The veneration accorded to the image is accepted by the Prototype. This is based on the Orthodox doctrine of *theosis* (deification): that is, true humanity is realized only in relationship with the divine prototype of humanness.

Prayer in worship does not include much silent prayer, that is, not audible moments of silence. Words are treated with great respect because Christ is the Word. All words, therefore, are an image of The Word. The respect is passed on. The words in the hymns and the prayers are taken from Christ or the saints. In the soul of a person, however, silence is valued. Hesychasm is the name given to this, and it is a form of prayer practised in hermit conditions. This inner stillness in the presence of God is highly venerated and one of the highest forms of prayer. Pure prayer is undisturbed by images or distractions. Active prayer, that of words, leads into wordless contemplative prayer in which the heart lays itself open in silence before God.

There is also an emphasis on self-condemnation, a lowly attitude towards oneself and avoiding self-admiration. 'It is higher to see your sins than to see an angel.' Confession, therefore, is a regular part of the life of prayer; to be without a spirit of repentance is dangerous. He who is humbled will be exalted. (Based on an essay by the Revd Maureen Green, 1996)

So the Christian worshipper sees before him not a celebrant but a screen of icons. The celebrant remains hidden behind the screen for most of the service, and the lay members contribute their own acts of worship. Some wander in late and leave early, some kneel, some stand. Each worships in his or her own way. The key reason behind this is a strong sense of the dwelling of the Holy Spirit in every Christian.

The screen of icons reminds the worshipper that, in Christ, man has become a link between the heavenly and earthly kingdoms. The royal doors, with their pictures of the Annunciation, declare that Christ alone is the door leading to communion with God. Through the royal door the priest brings the holy bread and wine, reminding us that Christ alone is the door leading to the presence of God.

In this communion Christians are closely linked with the great family of the living and departed. Death may rob us of sight but not of unity. So whenever the church is gathered together it does so in the presence of the saints and angels. Christians on earth join with the great company giving never-ceasing praise in glory. On entering a church, a candle is lit as a symbol of love and remembrance of those who have gone before.

Above the holy table is the tabernacle. In the Old Testament the ten commandments written by God were kept there. Now the consecrated bread and wine are stored there to remind us that God is ever present in his holy temple. Above the tabernacle the candle burns, reminding us that Christ is the light of the world.

The Gospel book is always placed on the holy table as another symbol of the presence of Christ, the Word of Life. The four Gospel writers, Matthew, Mark, Luke and John, are usually painted on the four corners of the dome to remind us that the gospel is for the whole world.

The pulpit is usually to the left in the nave. It is used for the reading of the Bible and sermons. It is made of stone to symbolize the stone used to seal Christ's tomb and from which the angel proclaimed the good news of the Resurrection – good news we still proclaim today.

Saints

The Greek word *hagios* which we translate as 'saint', comes from a word that means 'not like us, or different'. Saints are those who down the centuries have enabled others to see God shining through them. There is the story of a child looking up at a stained glass window and remarking: 'a saint is a Christian who lets God's light shine through.' To put it another way, as Paul wrote to the Corinthians, Christians are like the fragrance of the knowledge of him ... the aroma of Christ. All Christians should be that. Each of us should be becoming more like Jesus the more we let the Holy Spirit produce fruit in our life. So in the New Testament Paul describes Christians in Rome or Corinth as 'those called to be saints'. However, down the centuries the lives of certain Christians have been used as examples or models of how to live out the faith. They are saints with a capital 'S'. We often call churches after such persons: St Mary, St Peter, St James, St John to give just a few, and there are also local saints like St Edmund and St Alban who even have towns named after them.

It is important to remember that saints were not always perfect. They were human like us and the New Testament does not seek to cover up such failure. Peter denied Jesus, Mark deserted Paul and Barnabas when they left Cyprus to travel in Turkey.

Saints form an important part of the devotion in the Orthodox Church. It is recognized that there are far more saints, some known only to God, than we could ever honour in a special way, and most towns in the Orthodox world will hold a festival each year to remember a certain saint from their area.

There is a strong emphasis on being part of the family of God, the communion of saints, past, present and future. So it can be said, we know that when one falls, he falls alone; but no one is saved alone. He is saved in the church, as a member of her and in union with all her other members. From that follows teaching about the body of Christ, that Christ is never separated from his people. St John Chrysostom writes: 'Christ will be complete when his body has been completed.'

The saints in our daily life Seeing so many icons of saints, and seeing Orthodox Christians praying near those icons, causes us to ask about the role of saints in our Christian journey.

It is important to stress that they are on a different level from God. There is no question that there is only one mediator between God and man, Jesus Christ. Saints or Mary are never called upon in the sense of redeeming, saving, mediating. However, Hebrews talks of our being surrounded by a great cloud of witnesses and the Orthodox apply this to the saints with such statements as, 'We are surrounded by saints. The air is thick with them. They are like a great cloud enveloping us. They are with us as we run the race of life. They applaud and cheer us, they pray for us and have advice to give. They can tell us how they ran the race and won'. So Orthodox Christians may seek their prayers and their support. It is pointed out that it is strange if God hears the prayers of a Christian while on earth but not when with him in glory.

Orthodox Christians do not ask for the prayers of saints because they feel they are more human, understanding, and even accept a lower standard. That would call in question Christ's incarnate love for us. He is our High Priest able to sympathize with us in our weaknesses. So we can pray to Christ in great confidence, as is pointed out in Hebrews 4:15-16. However, it is possible to receive encouragement and strength from those who have faithfully lived for Christ in our own community or who have won through similar situations to the ones we face. Do they in glory pray for us and urge us on?

Veneration The Orthodox stress that they, therefore, never worship saints. Worship is only for God, but they do reverence them for they way they reflect Christ in our world. So the icons in the church and home are seen as a way in which we are caught up in our common journey with the saints. We are all part of the same body of Christ. In the early church a practice evolved of keeping the bones of the saints. When Polycarp, Bishop of Smyrna, was martyred in the second century it is recorded that the local Christians 'took up his bones, more valuable than precious stones and finer than gold, and laid them where it was fitting. There the Lord shall permit us, as shall be possible to us, to assemble ourselves together in joy and gladness, and to celebrate the birthday of his martyrdom, alike in memory of them that have fought before, and for the training and preparation of them that are to fight hereafter.' (*A New Eusebius,* J Stevenson, 1957, SPCK)

Saints of Greece

Various listings of national saints give Greece St Nicholas of Myra as the main patron saint, with St Andrew, St George and the Holy Mountain of our Lady (Mary the Mother of Jesus) also mentioned. Some maintain that such patron saints are a carrying over of the pagan gods, so Poseidon has become St Nicholas.

St Nicholas

St Nicholas was born in Patara in southern Turkey in a coastal area which even in Ottoman times was under Greek influence. His wealthy parents died of plague in his childhood. He inherited an estate which enabled him to make pilgrimages to Egypt and Palestine and carry out charitable work.

He was made bishop of the newly formed diocese of Myra by Constantine. At the Council of Nicea he is reputed to have physically attacked Arius. That may not have been his only fight, as his skull reveals that at some stage he broke his nose.

He died between AD 340 and 350. In the sixth century the church of St Nicholas was built round his tomb. The sarcophagus is still there, but the bones were taken in the eleventh century by sailors sent from Bari in Italy, to provide a relic to rival those of other Italian cities, like the bones of St Mark in Venice. It is said that upon smashing the lid of the tomb the thieves were almost overcome by the glowing bones and the powerful smell of myrrh. In 1862 Czar Alexander of Russia began a renovation of the church and further work has been carried out by the Turkish government.

His link with Santa Claus comes from a very early story that, on hearing that a shopkeeper was too poor to supply his daughters with dowries, he went by night and threw three bags of gold down the chimney or through the window or into the yard. At least by some means his gift saved the girls from a life of prostitution. Later these three golden bags or balls were used as the symbol of a pawnbroker's shop. It is thought that the idea of giving anonymous gifts was first adopted in the West by French nuns who left stockings for the poor, filled with fruit and nuts.

An internet article points out that St Nicholas, as the patron saint of Greece and Russia, features mainly in his role as the protector of sailors and seamen. 'At Christmas small fishing boats honour St Nicholas, especially in the islands, with decorations of blue and white lights. Tradition has it that his clothes are soaked with brine, his beard always dripping with seawater, and his face covered with perspiration because he has been fighting storms to reach sinking ships and save men from drowning.'

Greek ships carry an icon of St Nicholas, as he is regarded as master of wind and tempest. Sailors light a candle before the icon, praying for safe passage. When a ship is in danger the captain prays, making a solemn promise to bring a *tamata*, a Greek ex-voto (offering) of a small ship of silver, gold, or carved of wood, if they make port safely. On return from such a voyage, the captain and sailors take the ex-voto, representing their ship, to church. In thanksgiving for their safety, they place it before a St Nicholas icon. It is given as testimony to protection received, not as intercession for future aid.

Revered as the great protector, St Nicholas' feast is one of great devotion. The Greek Navy pays tribute to the patron saint of sailors with a special ceremony at the Hellenic Naval Academy.

Devotion to Saint Nicholas is also shown by the many small white chapels that dot the coastline. These chapels, dedicated to Saint Nicholas, have been built in gratitude to God for protection on the seas. As nearly every island family has members working in shipping, the navy, fishing or sponge diving, it is customary for folks passing one of these chapels to enter, light a candle, and pray for their friends' and relatives' protection from turbulent seas. Many families name a son 'Nikolaos' in honour of the saint.

St Nicholas is also part of Epiphany celebrations held by the sea. Priests bless ships anchored in harbour, in St Nicholas' name, asking him to watch over each one, bringing it safely through storms and back to harbour. Ships then blow their whistles and church bells ring as a cross is thrown into the water. Sailors dive to see who can retrieve the cross.

St Nicholas the Wonderworker is also called upon to preside in spirit over Orthodox meetings seeking unity among churches.

St Andrew

The apostle is shared with Romania, Russia, Scotland and the Ukraine. He is usually depicted with the St Andrew's cross and with a fish. He is regarded in Greece as the patron saint of fishermen, spinsters, infertile wives, weddings and sore throats!

Andrew, the elder brother of St Peter, came from Bethsaida in Galilee. Jesus called him from his trade as a fisherman. He was one of the four closest disciples to Jesus in his earthly ministry. He first appears when he introduces Peter to Jesus (John1:40-42) and then when Jesus called the four fishermen (Matt. 4:18-22). He is listed among the chosen twelve disciples (Matt. 10:2-4, et al). He is mentioned in the feeding of the 5,000 (John 6:8-9); when Greeks came to see Jesus (John 12:20-22); on the Mount of Olives (Mark 13:3-4); and in the upper room (Acts1:12-14). It is claimed that, after Pentecost, Andrew preached in Turkey and Greece before he was crucified at Patra in Achaia.

Various legends have arisen about him. It is claimed that his bones were kept in Constantinople until 1210 and that a relic can still be found in St Andrew's Cephalonia (a large island on the west side of Greece). Among the popular stories is one which tells of him sailing to Murgundia where he found St Matthew in prison and in terrible pain. Andrew entered through the prison doors, which opened for him, and healed St Matthew. The local people hailed him as a wonder worker and accepted the Christian faith. Another legend tells us that St Andrew had a young nobleman from Antioch following him against the parents' wishes. They tried to burn the house where the two men resided, but the saint put the fire out with a glass of water.

St George

Greece holds St George as a major patron saint along with England, Ethiopia, Georgia, Germany, Lithuania, Malta, Moldova, Montenegro, Portugal, Russia and Serbia.

St George was martyred in Lydda, Palestine around AD 300. He is thought to have been from Cappadocia and an officer in the Roman army. He refused to make a sacrifice to the emperor and was imprisoned. It is said that the emperor ordered he be given poison to drink but it did not affect him. Other attempts to kill him were defeated by angels until he finally was given the honour of martyrdom. The legend of the dragon is Italian, around the time of the crusades.

In it St George is supposed to have saved the daughter of the king of Libya. He is considered to be a special helper against the plague, leprosy, snakebites and witches. He also avenges women who seek his help.

The Greek alphabet

Name	capital	lower case	like English
Alpha	A	α	a
Beta	B	β	b
Gamma	Γ	γ	g
Delta	Δ	δ	d
Epsilon	E	ε	e
Zeta	Z	ζ	z
Eta	H	η	e as in fete
Theta	Θ	θ	th
Iota	I	ι	i
Kappa	K	κ	k
Lambda	Λ	λ	l
Mu	M	μ	m
Nu	N	ν	n
Xi	Ξ	ξ	x
Omicron	O	o	o
Pi	Π	π	p
Rho	P	ρ	r
Sigma	Σ	σ ←	**s**
Tau	T	τ	t
Upsilon	Y	υ	u
Phi	Φ	φ	ph
Chi	X	χ	ch
Psi	Ψ	ψ	ps
Omega	Ω	ω	o as in tone

Glossary

Acropolis	The fort built on a hill above the town
Aedicula	Small temple-like structure for a shrine or the columns supporting an arch over a niche or window
Agora	Marketplace
Amphitheatre	Oval or circular with seats rising all round a central stage
Apse	Semicircular east end of a basilica/church
Cavea	The subterranean cells for keeping wild animals but sometimes used for the amphitheatre itself
Cupola	Hemispherical roof
Diazoma	Upper walkway of a theatre with doorways leading to passageways
Hippodrome	Stadium used for chariot racing or other sports
Hypocaust	System of underfloor heating by means of hot air in pipes
Narthex	Large porch to basilica usually stretching the full width of the church
Nymphaeum	Building adorned with flowing water, plants and a sanctuary
Palaestra	Gymnasium
Parados	Mound of earth to secure a fortified place from attack often behind a trench
Pendentive	A spherical triangle formed by the intersection of a dome by two pairs of opposite arches springing from supporting columns
Politeuma	Quasi-independent community
Portico	Columns supporting a pediment

Propylon	(Greek: before gate) An entrance or vestibule to a temple or group of buildings
Prytaneum	Public hall
Sarcophagus	Stone coffin (Greek: flesh eating) often with sculptures and inscriptions
Stoa	Colonnaded walk with blank rear and side walls
Stylobate	A continuous base supporting rows of columns
Theatre	Formed, often from a hillside, as a segment of a circle
Trapezoidal	Quadrilateral with no parallel sides

Notes

Notes

Notes

Notes